NO COMPROMISE

NO COMPROMISE
Selected Writings
of
Karl Kraus

Edited, and with an introduction, by
Frederick Ungar

FREDERICK UNGAR PUBLISHING CO.
New York

Translators

Sheema Z. Buehne, Edward Mornin, Helene Scher, Marcus Bullock,
Michael Bullock, Frederick Ungar, D. G. Wright

Library of Congress Cataloging in Publication Data

Kraus, Karl, 1874–1936.
  No compromise.

  Bibliography: p.
  I. Title.
PT2621.R27A235   1977   838'.9'1209   76–15653
ISBN 0–8044–2485–3

If there is a wall of silence around me,
I will make the silence audible!

Karl Kraus

Contents

Introduction

Karl Kraus is no longer entirely unknown to American readers, as he was only a few years ago. His importance has been increasingly recognized, and there have been several worthwhile publications* in English on his life and work. Other widely reviewed books treating of the Vienna of Kraus's time have also helped to create new interest in this greatest satirist of the twentieth century.

But Kraus was more than an outstanding satirist. He was one of the finest writers of all time in the German language—aphorist, essayist, poet, culture critic, dramatist. Above all, he was a fighter without peer against corruption of any kind, in particular the corruption of language and the trivialization of life. His work and personality exerted a profound influence on such diverse figures as Ludwig Wittgenstein and Arnold Schönberg and other great minds of his time.

* *The Last Days of Mankind: Karl Kraus and His Vienna* by Frank Field (1967); *Karl Kraus* by Harry Zohn (1971); *The Last Days of Mankind* by Karl Kraus, abridged and edited by Frederick Ungar (1974).

1

Kraus belonged to a generation that could still sense traces of an aura that enveloped a past long gone. A quite different era was to follow. Technology, that most potent tool of industrial capitalism, had ushered in a new materialistic world. Rapid technological changes, added to the miscarried revolution of 1848—a turning point in the political and cultural development of Austria—brought to the fore people of a different type whose desire to achieve quick material success became more and more pronounced.

Up to the middle of the nineteenth century the Austrians, not unlike the peoples of the ancient world, still enjoyed naively the good things in life. Their spirit was earthy and life-affirming despite the social ills inherent in an authoritarian regime that feared nothing more than political liberalization and enlightenment. The ruling Hapsburgs pursued their own dynastic interests, supported by an oligarchy of speculators and their journalistic henchmen whose influence was all-pervasive.

Karl Kraus was born on April 28, 1874, in Jičin, Moravia. His father, a prosperous paper manufacturer, soon moved the family to Vienna, where Kraus lived for the rest of his life. In deference to his father's wishes he enrolled in the Law School of the University of Vienna but soon turned to philosophical and Germanistic studies. But it was the theater that increasingly captured his interest. He tried his hand at directing and also at acting in amateur performances, but soon realized that a slight physical handicap—the result mainly of a minor curvature of the spine—would make it difficult for him to succeed as an actor. Nevertheless, he had a great theatrical talent, with a subtle awareness of intonation and an extraordinary ability to imitate voices. He was appalled to see dramatic works poorly performed in Vienna and decided to present them with greater artistry himself in public recitals. The plays chosen were mainly works of Shakespeare, Goethe, Nestroy, and Raimund, the latter two quintessentially Viennese. These he presented, along with readings of his own works, in the 701 recitals he gave until his death in 1936.

As a student Kraus contributed theater and book reviews to several literary periodicals. He published his first longer work, *Die demolierte Literatur* (The Demolished Literature) in the *Wiener Rundschau* (Vienna Review) in 1896. This satire, appearing in book form the following year, led to the young writer's becoming favorably known. In 1898 Kraus became editor of the magazine *Die Waage* (The Scales), for which he wrote critical pieces on politics and on cultural aspects of public life. His position gave him an insider's view of the extent to which truth in journalism is inhibited by political, financial, and social considerations. A man of independent means, he decided to escape all restrictions on his writing by establishing his own publication in 1899. *Die Fackel* (The Torch), which became his main weapon in a lifelong battle against the press, appeared irregularly at first, in brief single issues on the average of once a month, but sometimes several times a month. Later it appeared in much longer issues at intervals of several months.

We have a report by the Austrian writer Robert Scheu on the reaction to the first issue of *Die Fackel*: "Vienna has never experienced such a day! What a whispering, tingling, prickling excitement. In the streets, on the trams, in the city park, everybody reading a red brochure. . . . It was madness! The little brochure, for which a sale of only a few hundred copies was originally expected, had to have a new printing of ten thousand copies within a few days."

During its first twelve years, *Die Fackel* published contributions by statesmen (Thomas G. Masaryk, Heinrich Lamasch), public figures (Karl Liebknecht, Viktor Adler), and writers (August Strindberg, Frank Wedekind, Oscar Wilde, Heinrich

Mann, Peter Altenberg, Georg Trakl), people whose views or work Kraus esteemed and wanted to further. From 1911 on, however, up to his death on June 12, 1936, *Die Fackel* was written entirely by Kraus himself. It was, in a sense, an autobiographical diary; it is the history of his life.

The pages of *Die Fackel* set high ethical and artistic standards. Kraus attacked venality in government and corruption everywhere, especially in the press, his main target throughout his life. The Austrian press, at first an innocuous means of distributing news, had since 1848 become a powerful and sinister tool, reflecting the commercialization of public life; it often dominated public opinion. Internal stresses within the empire offered the press a unique opportunity. The Hapsburg rulers were compelled, by the "Ausgleich" (Compromise) of 1867, to grant wide autonomy to the Hungarians, the most highly organized and politically effective nationality within the empire and one which had struggled for many years for independence. One result of the compromise was that half the empire—the populations of Transylvania, Slovakia, Ruthenia, Slovenia, Croatia, and the Banat—was brought under Hungarian rule and treated even more harshly than before.

The long drawn-out struggle for a constitutional settlement, the perpetual strain between the government in Vienna and Budapest, national and religious differences among the multinational population of the Austro-Hungarian empire, all presented the press with an excellent chance to put down firm roots and make itself indispensable. Under the guise of freedom, equality, and enlightenment the press masqueraded as the savior of the fatherland, the protagonist of freedom of thought, the bulwark of the commonweal. In actuality it was at all times the pliable tool of commercial-industrial interests.

Journalism became the target of Kraus's bitterest attacks. To him journalism was the embodiment of intellectual venality.

Was it not August Zang, the founder in 1864 of the *Neue Freie Presse*, the leading organ of the liberal bourgeoisie in the Austrian part of the empire, who stated as his ideal arrangement that every single column of his paper be paid for by outside interests? And were the goals of Moriz Benedikt, his successor, very different?

Among the Viennese newspapers the *Neue Freie Presse* was the most influential; it was often considered the mouthpiece of the government, which in turn was at times dependent on the paper's goodwill. Combining its financial corruption with journalistic excellence, it counted among its occasional contributors such literary personalities as Hugo von Hofmannsthal, Arthur Schnitzler, and Richard Beer-Hofmann. Moriz Benedikt, the newspaper's chief editor and part owner, seemed to Kraus to be the incarnation of evil. He appears as one of the characters in *The Last Days of Mankind* (Act I, Scene 28, included here). He is also portrayed in the Epilogue of that drama (not included here) as the Lord of the Hyenas.

Kraus was not the first to recognize and fight the pernicious activity of the press of his time, which showed journalism in its ugliest form, but he was its most persistent and most implacable enemy. He pinpointed and attacked abuses in politics, in the administration of justice, as well as in art and literature, as they were presented in the press. He held the press accountable for these abuses because it was the press that aided and abetted the all but universal corruption. This battle seemed for him to be the central purpose of his life.

He was not alone in his attacks on the press. Among Kraus's contemporaries was Josef Schöffel, the savior of the Vienna Woods, whose exchange of letters with Kraus is included in this volume. Sören Kierkegaard, the nineteenth-century Danish philosopher of religion, was a still more embittered foe of journalism. In his public readings Kraus more than once quoted

Kierkegaard's contemptuous condemnations of journalism. "Woe, woe, the daily press! If Christ were to live now, he would take aim, as sure as I live, not at high priests but at journalists." Another is included in the essay "Écrasez l'infâme!", presented in this volume. Several other selections (see below) demonstrate Kraus's fury at the hypocrisy and evil of the press. Many of these biting satirical attacks are also very witty.

The press was aware that it had no defense against Kraus's satiric arrows and knew that it could not oppose him as an equal adversary. It saw its best defense in ignoring his attacks, and it reacted by surrounding him with a wall of silence. "Even if a comet were to graze my head," Kraus wrote, "the papers would not report its appearance." Kraus repeatedly took issue with this policy of silence, mocking its ineffectiveness. Several examples of this famous war against the press are included here—"Self-Admiration," "Bread and Lies," and replies to libel suits brought against Kraus. The reception of his public readings—always sold out—also proved the press blackout to be in vain. Without more than the posting of an announcement on the wall of a concert hall, Kraus always filled the hall to capacity. The proceeds were given to charity. No one, in or out of journalism, could match him in a polemical feud, and few dared to try.

The official world of literature also refused to take notice of Kraus. He had attacked its lack of moral fiber too forcefully, particularly its disgraceful attitude during World War I, when he was the only writer of rank to voice a fiery protest. Literary historians of his time, who did not fail to deal with the writings of even quite minor talents, were not ashamed to ignore Kraus, whose fame "sounded louder than if the press gang had everyday carried me in their dirty mouths."

The great wall of silence continued to envelop Kraus even

after the end of the war, dissipating only after his death. Then, and after the collapse of the Third Reich in 1945, all his books were republished, including the thirty-seven volumes comprising all issues of *Die Fackel* he had brought out since 1899. Kraus is now one of the writers most frequently quoted in Austria and Germany.

From a kind of Viennese muckraker-gadfly in the first years of *Die Fackel*, Kraus soon developed into a profound critic, not only of the press but of society and culture in general. His polemics against the perversion of public life turned into satire on a grand scale. Placing reality with its shortcomings against the ideal as the highest reality, Kraus saw satire as springing from a passionate desire for the lost ideal image of every debased object. It is the mission of genuine satire to eradicate what is rotten so that there may be room for what Kraus calls "der Schöpfung ihre Ehre zu erweisen" (to bestow honor on creation) by leading man back to an unspoiled pristine state, the "Ursprung" (source), a concept that plays such a large role in his poetry. Kraus knew well that the "Ursprung" had never existed, yet he felt it as part of his early youth, as a remnant of a not too distant past whose echoes he could still sense. The concept is central to his thinking. The "Ursprung" is the lost world of the first day, the day on which God gave man his first law, the world that was lost through man's sins. It is for the poet to re-create this world in his poetry. Kraus does so also in his satire, in which he destroys the world as it is and thus preserves the world of the "source." Satire thus forms a unity with poetry, which also points to the ideal, although by other means.

Kraus's characteristic method of satire was to present a quotation followed by his own comment. But even without a comment the very publication of a quoted article in *Die Fackel* changed its nature. "I must only quote the praises sung them, and it turns into the most vicious attack. . . . I take honey from dripping lips, and lo, it is pitch."

Kraus's approach to life was esthetic and ethical, and his yardstick the absolute. That has its irrational aspects; life, after all, cannot avoid compromise. With his unbending standards Kraus could not long identify with any political party and varied his allegiance with the ethical demands of the issue under consideration, alternately heaping scorn on all sectors of the political spectrum. Because no compromise was acceptable that conflicted with his moral sense, Kraus was often unjust and overly harsh with those he attacked, never giving thought to the consequences for his victims or the motivations of their actions. Lest we ourselves be guilty of the same human weakness and disregard extenuating circumstances, we must remember that Kraus acted out of a moral commitment he regarded as higher than any consideration for the person involved.

The accusation of anti-Semitism has often been leveled against Kraus. With equal justice the prophets of the Old Testament could have been so accused for castigating the Israelites who worshiped the Golden Calf. Born into a Jewish family, Kraus was highly sensitive to the moral conduct of Jews, particularly journalists. He considered Jewish journalists more talented, and therefore more dangerous, than their gentile colleagues—an accurate observation in the Vienna of his time. He actually berated them for being better at nourishing anti-Semitism than combatting it. Yet Kraus affirms, speaking of himself, that "in reverence to ravished life and befouled language he is gratefully aware of the vital strength of an uncompromisable Judaism he deeply loves. He sees it as resting in itself, quite untroubled by race and class and by any kind of hatred between troglodytes and profiteers."

Despite his eagerness to assimilate to German culture, despite his hatred for the forces of materialism with which so many Jewish intellectuals associated themselves—forces hostile to esthetic and spiritual values—Kraus in many ways remained intensely Jewish. His vision of language was the specifically Jewish concept of the revelation of the will of God through the word, the word that brings to pass what it says. Kraus's relationship to language was of a magical and religious character. He firmly believed in a preestablished harmony of word and world. He had the gift of letting the spirit of language, as it were, think for him, and would then follow it into the labyrinth like a somnambulist. "I have drawn out of language many a thought I did not have or could not put into words." Language for him was the divining rod that locates the springs of thought, the key to bringing order out of chaos.

Kraus elevated language, which he believed to be a direct index of morality, to man's essential concern, to which every other consideration should be subordinated. In the way language is used, he saw the cultural strength or weakness of a nation and the carrier of its spirit. He firmly believed that purification of language would in turn help to purify ethics. Purity of language was thus for him the measure of a man's integrity. He championed the honor of language by dishonoring the culpable speaker.

It is significant that the major part of the essays and letters included here were written during or soon after World War I. Most of the letters are directed to, received from, or refer to participants in the war or to profiteers and their victims. These were Kraus's finest hours. In the words of Walter Muschg, the Swiss literary historian: "With the outbreak of war in 1914, Kraus's art transcended itself. From being Viennese it rose to become universal, from being literary it became religious. The heritage of high Jewish spirituality, dormant in Kraus in his younger years, came to life. . . . Kraus is a spirit who acts under higher orders."

The aphorism is an art form to which Kraus felt particularly attracted and in which his sparkling wit is given full play. His special fascination with aphorisms led to the creation of several thousand, most of them before World War I. These were collected in *Sprüche und Widersprüche,* 1909 (Sayings and Counter Sayings) and *Pro Domo et Mundo,* 1912 (from the Latin, For Home and World). The earlier aphorisms were characterized by a youthful lightheartedness absent from the third and last collection, written in part during the war. Its symbolic title, *Nachts,* 1918 (At Night), pointed both to Kraus's own working night-time habits and to the darkness closing in on the world. The prewar aphorisms, which stem from Kraus's aesthetic and erotic period, do not provide a representative over-all picture of Kraus's work in this field and are therefore not amply included in this volume.

Not all pieces in this section are, strictly speaking, aphorisms, some having been detached from their original context; but they can clearly stand on their own. No uniform world view can be derived from the sum of these aphorisms. Kraus was not a systematic thinker, nor did he wish to be one. Many of his aphorisms, among them some of the best, are untranslatable. The idiomatic character of Kraus's writing here, with its nimble verbal acrobatics, resists any attempt at translation.

With his last volume, *Nachts,* Kraus's aphoristic period came to an end. His creative powers were now directed at a new field. Kraus was a poet of high order, who left behind an extensive body of poetry in the nine-volume *Worte in Versen* (Words in Verse). He started to write poetry when the horrors of the war era drove him to seek the timeless realm of nature and of love and of his central experience—the mystery of language. The meter and rhyme are traditional, yet he is a lyric poet of strong dramatic effect. In one of his poems Kraus calls himself an "epigone," by which he meant, however, not an undistinguished imitator of a great poet but rather one who conservatively guards a great tradition with which he identifies. Many of Kraus's poems are cerebral, their content often identical with his militant prose. Yet his oeuvre contains examples of great lyric power in which beauty of language and emotional content merge in perfect harmony. He never married, but some of the poems of great warmth or passion reflect his deep and lasting friendship with the Baroness Sidonie Nadherny von Borutin, at whose family estate near Prague he often spent the summer months.

The climax of Kraus's work was the epic drama *The Last Days of Mankind*. An immense achievement, it builds to an apocalyptic warning of impending world-engulfing disaster. It was written throughout the war years, when Kraus's voice was almost the only one raised against the general war enthusiasm. Never for a moment did he succumb to the chauvinistic poison that filled the air in those years. *The Last Days of Mankind* speaks to today's readers as if from the more recent past. In a truly prophetic vision it anticipates atomic armament and its catastrophic consequences for mankind.

In the drama seemingly unconnected occurrences are developed on two alternating levels. On one hand, Kraus presents the cruelties, inhumanity, and banality of life at the front and at home by means of a stunning variety of characters and situations; on the other, in dialogues of a fundamental nature between the Grumbler and the Optimist as well as the Subscriber and the Patriot, Kraus tries to bring sense to what is senseless and at least to suggest the search for a rational point of view.

To a large extent the text of *The Last Days* consists of quotations—words that were actually spoken or written. It is in a way the first documentary drama. Kraus was convinced that a speaker's self-unmasking by way of quotation was more devastating than direct attack. In scenes of biting scorn and in gigantic visions of horror he portrayed the monstrousness of war. A more powerful denunciation of war has never been written. The lack of unity of time, place, and action makes the unity of the *idea* the more compelling. "This book," wrote Alfred H. Fried, pacifist and a winner of the Nobel Peace Prize, "will have to be read by those who want to work against war. I count it among the noblest creations of the mind. It belongs among those books of mankind that are of eternal value."

A word about the selections in this volume. With the exception of a few poems, all pieces are taken from *Die Fackel.* I have endeavored to choose out of the thirty thousand pages of Kraus's writings, which represent his total oeuvre, those most characteristic of his work, those that were closest to his heart and mind. They are also those that he read with particular gusto at his public recitals more often than others. These recitals were unforgettable experiences. As a Viennese myself, and as a young publisher in the city, I missed very few of Kraus's readings.

A number of omissions in the text, some quite drastic, proved to be necessary, and this for compelling reasons. Untranslatability has notoriously been the hallmark of Kraus's work, the reason it remained unknown for so long to most English-speaking readers. The abridged English edition of *The Last Days of Mankind,* published to mark the centennial anniversary of Kraus's birth, at least qualified this preconception. But the difficulties of translation are indeed very great. They stem not only from Kraus's ingenious play on words, double meanings, special connotations of words and phrases; an additional difficulty is that there are no English equivalents for many German terms reflecting the different structures of Austrian/German society, systems of government, social customs, etc. Furthermore, the length of some of the selections would not hold the attention of readers unfamiliar with the time and place involved. It would have been a disservice to Kraus as well as the reader if the principle of absolute completeness of text, desirable as it normally is, had prevailed in this volume. Ellipsis marks indicating omissions are not used so that a more readable text may be achieved.

Karl Kraus died when Austria was facing the menace of National Socialism at its western borders, two years before the forced Anschluss of 1938. The outbreak of barbarism in neighboring Germany may have precipitated his death. His final work, written during this time, was not published until 1952. Through an analysis of language and speech, *Die dritte Walpurgisnacht* (The Third Walpurgisnight) portrays the horror of the Hitler era, his dictatorship, and its literary henchmen. It is a perceptive exploration of the diabolical nature of the Third Reich.

During his lifetime the impact of Kraus's work was largely restricted to Vienna. Since the end of World War II his importance and his influence have been widely acknowledged within German letters, though as yet not in full proportion to his extraordinary contribution to the artistic and intellectual life of his age. Although Kraus's writings condemned his time, although he foresaw prophetically the dangers inherent in modern civilization, his work in its totality is nonetheless a profession of faith in man and in the worth of life. It was his deep confidence that his work would endure:

> . . . fort zu leben, wenn ich abgeschieden.
> (to live on when I am gone to the shadows.)

The life work of Karl Kraus was not only a great ethical and artistic achievement, to which he sacrificed his peace and outer success; it was also a refuge, one of the few remaining, of basic human values and threatened human dignity. His torch illuminated the darkness. May it be held aloft and handed on!

FREDERICK UNGAR

ESSAYS

Initials

[1908]

O.G.Z.B.D.G. That's what it was called. I found the mysterious initials in the return address of the envelope of a letter that came through the mail. This is exactly how Belshazzar must have felt when a finger began to write on the wall. But even a Daniel would have tried in vain to decipher this enigmatic inscription. O.G.Z.B.D.G. Something was about to happen to me. Hesitantly I inspected the letter. Weighed in the balance and found wanting? To put an end to the terrible uncertainty, I decided to open the letter.

It turned out that the finger in question was that of a specialist in venereal diseases, who felt it necessary in the interest of public health to cry out to the sinners of this world: O.G.Z.B.D.G. Unceasingly he cried out. His cries penetrated the palaces of the rich and the cottages of the poor, and wherever two ill-advised people were on the point of following the call of nature his cry was stronger than that call. O.G.Z.B.D.G.! Only later did it become clear to me that what was at issue here was nothing less than the founding of an Oesterreichische Gesellschaft zur Bekämpfung der Geschlechtskrankheiten—

Austrian Society for the Prevention of Venereal Disease. The moment I saw the discreet initials chosen by this fighting organization, what immediately came to mind was Oeffentliche Geneigtheit zur Bewahrung des Geheimnisses—Public Tendency to Preserve Secrecy. I was merely in doubt as to whether these initials might not stand for Oeffentliche Gelegenheit zum Beweise der Geistlosigkeit—Public Opportunity for the Demonstration of Idiocy. But when I learned that the organization was planning to conduct a joint study, all I could think of was Oesterreichische Geneigtheit zur Betätigung der Geschaftlhuberei—Austrian Tendency to Indulge in Busybody-ness. And lo and behold, this interpretation also brought me close to the true meaning of the initials.

It was in fact an association whose members were called upon by its statutes to prevent the incidence of any venereal disease. I had all the greater sympathy with the aims of this organization as I was persuaded by the newspaper articles published by its board, for propaganda purposes, that it was indeed on the only right road by which to reach its goal of wiping out venereal disease. The board started from the premise that the only sure way to put an end to it was by practicing abstinence and leading a blameless life. Nothing, I thought, could be more logical and incontestable, since scientific experiments had shown that the origin of syphilis was to be found in sexual intercourse. Only prudery and false shame could have stopped the board from revealing to the world the one and only sure means of avoiding infection.

Of course, much as one might approve the viewpoint leading to this action, one nevertheless had to consider the difficulties standing in its way and admit that the world had unfortunately not reached the height of such truth. For people may be hypocritical enough to became supporting but not practicing members of a society that propagates such valuable information as the advantages of abstinence. From the outset I feared that the idealistic aspirations of this organization would be frustrated by public resistance.

But the O.G.Z.B.D.G. refused to be discouraged and, in order to demonstrate to the widest possible audience the practicality of the chosen method, has set in motion the inquiry in question, in which the most competent and professionally best trained upholders of morality were to try to persuade the public to leave the field to venereal disease, since a retreat on the latter's part was out of the question. Even less, however, was any help to be expected from science, which for the time being could not but scorn joining issue with an adversary whose power rested upon immorality.

To my satisfaction, I learned from the invitation I had been sent that, although they had never harbored any hope of gaining me as a member, they attached all the greater importance to having my views as those of an expert on the subject. Both facts flattered my vanity, but above all I felt that they saw in me the writer who had the everlasting merit of having been the first, in an age that dared to have venereal disease but not to name it, to utter the word "syphilis." For up till then it had been considered an illness in which discretion was a point of honor, indeed the main point, and the newspapers maintained silence about it as if it were a stock swindle. If, then, a veil of silence had previously been cast over syphilis, it seemed that now it was to be banished by talking about it. If people previously sinned in secret, now they were to practice abstinence in the full glare of publicity.

The new method of eliminating the evil was by far the more radical. For if rain is coming through the roof, that unfortunate situation is surely more readily remedied by demolishing the house than by keeping the flooding a secret. But if, to be on the safe side, the occupants of the house are allowed to die out, one can be fairly certain to eliminate the calamity altogether. Hence the plan to deliver the death blow to syphilis, not by combatting the disease but by preventive measures against sexuality, would in no way have deterred me from taking part in the inquiry. On the contrary, I was all the more sympathetic toward the project because the extinction of humanity will inevitably also bring with it the extinction of stupidity and, as a further consequence, nip in the bud any inquiry into the prevention of venereal disease. But, unfortunately, I absolutely could not approve of the manner in which the O.G.Z.B.D.G. was setting about the propagation of its aims.

After the tactful way in which the society had introduced itself on the envelope containing the invitation, one might have expected it to rest content with recommending abstinence and not to have publicized these already sufficiently widespread diseases in a manner grossly offending the modesty of newspaper readers. In no case can one approve when medical specialists are seized with journalistic ambitions and apply to gonorrhea the kind of scribbling cure that by its very nature conflicts with confidentiality. To be sure, I found that in an article published as an exhortation to humanity by the society the author discreetly omitted the names of the infections against which he was warning, referring to them simply as "a particular group of diseases." But to make up for this, he went on to complain of the hypocrisy of society, which for ridiculous reasons of propriety did not even dare to refer to them by name.

Now, hypocrisy is certainly an even more dangerous infectious disease, to which even physicians are not immune, and the author was not afraid to name it. We further learned that arthritis, peritonitis, and puerperal fever are the consequences of "another illness," but this illness had to rest content with being described merely as "one of the diseases that concern us

here." Unfortunately, the author did not maintain his beneficent restraint when he came to speak of the second of the diseases that concern us here. Since he considered it necessary to abandon a prudish standpoint in these matters, he allowed himself to be carried away into revealing to us—fortunately not until the conclusion of the article—the word "syphilis."

This indiscretion wounded my susceptibilities to such an extent that I could not bring myself to place my expertise at the disposal of the O.G.Z.B.D.G. And the course of the joint study was such that it only reinforced my distrust. I myself was to have spoken on the subject of "Sexual Enlightenment," but I preferred to decline because I had good reason to fear that I would give offense by a discussion of precisely this question. "Nothing is further from my mind," I wrote, "than to underestimate its vital significance. I am a friend of enlightenment, but what I consider necessary to say on the subject I have already said often enough, and I could only repeat how essential I consider it that children should finally introduce parents to the mysteries of sexual life. For dark and tortuous are the paths along which it leads, and how often does not an adult stumble!"

In any case, I doubted whether my contribution to the inquiry would ever be read in public. It would wrongly be taken for the expression of a cynical outlook on life. Yet I know that the future will acknowledge me right. Assuming, of course, that mankind, if it accepts the propaganda for chastity, has any future. But even now we can see instances every day where the inexperience of the adult leads. If the initiators of the inquiry had allowed themselves to be enlightened in time by their children as to how urgent the sexual impulse is in human beings, it would never have occurred to them to initiate an inquiry. For although, according to Wilhelm Busch, abstinence is the pleasure in things we cannot have, it is unbelievable how pleasure-seeking the world in general is. People would rather catch venereal diseases than forego their cause, for it is still easier to be cured of them than of the inclination unintentionally to catch them. Anyhow, that softening of the brain is connected with syphilis they learn from the minutes of those inquiries in which avoidance of enjoyment is recommended as a protection against the danger. But venereal diseases are no more apt to be scared by morality congresses than by medical conferences that turn out to be morality congresses. The world reads O.G.Z.B.D.G. and hopes the Oertliche Gelegenheit zur Betätigung des Geschlechtstriebes—the Local Opportunity for Gratifying the Sexual Impulse—will finally be revealed to it. For it is this that is constantly being blocked by a fence of laws or the thorny hedge of morality. If the world should now, out of fear of venereal diseases, forego the view of Venus, it would become dejected. But we do not want sadness to precede lust and lust then not to follow. The medical specialists will perhaps give us useful service in their offices. But if they prescribe abstinence, then there is more joy in heaven over a sinner who does not repent than over one hundred righteous who get somewhere.

TRANSLATED BY MICHAEL BULLOCK

Self-Admiration
[1908]

"... thus he has so long to subsist on his own approval until
that of the world follows it. Until then even his own approval is
spoiled for him in that he is expected to be nicely modest. It is,
however, as impossible for someone who has merit and knows
its cost to be blind to it himself as for a man six feet tall not to
notice that he towers above the others ..."
Schopenhauer, The World as Will and Idea

"Self-admiration is permissible if the self is beautiful. It becomes an obligation if the reflecting mirror is a good one."
Kraus, Sprüche und Widersprüche

That I accept the reproach of self-admiration as the observation
of a character trait well known to me and that I respond, not
with contrition, but by continuing the provocation—this my
readers should know by now. Naturally, I do not do this
in defiance, nor even for my own benefit. In speaking about
myself, I aim neither to offend nor to please anyone. Rather, as
a representative of Austrian intellectual life I simply wish to
guard against the danger of its being said some day that no

one here in Austria ever talked about me. Viennese intellectuals ought to be grateful to me for having taken the trouble off their shoulders and preserved their reputation. Why should I not admit that delight at a word of appreciation makes me want to repeat it? Whoever gladly dispenses with praise from the multitude, will not deny himself the chance to be his own partisan. Imagination has the right to revel in the paltriest shade of the tree out of which it makes a forest. There exists no reproach more ridiculous than that of vanity, if it is conscious of itself. I take the liberty of giving to myself all the pleasures of the cliques. Not even the most malicious idiot will believe I set great store on being the darling of the Viennese critics and am complaining because I am not. But to assert that they are hiding their respect for me, which grows greater by the day, behind the cowardly mask of convention, and that they do not open their mouths even when they would like to speak, is a task incumbent on me just then when I am considered to be merely a watchdog for the corrupt machinations of a city. What would I gain from this silence if I did not make it audible? It would be a poor retort not to talk about it.

The citing of opinions from outside Austria, however, also confirms a universal aesthetic insight. Such opinions indicate the distance foreign readers have toward a work that grows from current or accidental, almost always insignificant incidents into an artistic structure with a distinct perspective. In the city in which the works were written, the incidents are too well known for the readers to appreciate their artistic presentation. This distinction seems to suggest that here also enhanced comprehension will depend on diminished topicality and that distance in time will have the same effect on local readers as distance in space already has on foreign readers and that my writings need only go out of date in order to become up to date also in Vienna.

Such hopes are justified above all by the headshaking with which many greeted my "personal" publications, even on the part of such readers who concede the right to surprises once and for all to an author who publishes his diary as a periodical. Of course, from one who looks only for the actual target of aphoristic remarks I expect only the question "who" is the target. I answer: I myself, nobody but me!

Readers who take a love poem for an address and the satirical portrayal of a type for an attack I cannot please and do not want to. Others again know the accidental target for my self-laceration—in that case their interest in the specific subject matter is satisfied to such an extent that they become blind to the perspective, even if they might otherwise be capable of appreciating it. They concede, at least in principle, that a dramatist has the right to overrate the most insignificant real-life person and make use of his peculiarities if they seem fruitful for the artistic portrayal of the typical. But in practice such readers still respond as if it were a play *à clef*. They see only the portrait of the person familiar to them, misjudge the artistic achievement that ought to obliterate all memory of an indifferent model, and believe that "too much honor" has been done it.

Only those readers who neither seek nor know the incident can fully appreciate the expression of anger or love. They do not demand that one sing the praises of a queen or that blame be meted out to a king; they judge the poem itself, whether a fool, male or female, be its subject. After all, no sensitive person must be denied the right to be inspired by the most insignificant stimulus; and analyzing the stimulus, if the inspiration was good, is a method that kills any artistic venture. Whoever takes aphorisms for mere polemics may take for a play *à clef* any drama in which he happens to know the concrete allusions. Polemics presuppose notoriety of the evil and demand congru-

ity of fictitious character and real person. But I have never let
the fear of making the target well known or popular deprive
me of my pleasure in the satirical portrayal of experiences that,
objectively speaking, mean only little. I have always done too
much honor to the most trivial incident.

Whoever does not like such subjective arbitrariness may
avoid the author, but he does not have the right in every single
case to chide him for his consistency. It should altogether surprise no one that I give personal matters a personal form; and
to blame me for putting myself in the center of my own experiences is an impropriety I do not deserve. The long-eared
faithful reader who adds up for me how many times "I" and
"my" occur in a publication—and I am not such a jackass as to
want to justify its appearance in print—is, of course, correct
from his point of view. I just fail to comprehend why he is in-
discreet enough to stick his nose into someone else's diary.
That I am arrogant enough to have it printed does not by any
means justify such curiosity. Reflections about current affairs
are not to be found in it, and the useful activity of cleaning imperial façades cannot be expected from me. To be sure, no "I"
would be involved in that kind of work. Yet people who are
not involved with me and those who live abroad do not measure the merit of my literary creations by their subject matter,
which here constitutes the sole justification of my existence, but
recognize literary merit exactly because they are far removed
from the subject matter.

No writer has ever made vanity easier for his reader to discover than I have. For even if he did not notice himself that I
am vain, he learned it from my repeated admissions of vanity
and from the unrestrained approval I lavished on this vice. The
informed smile at the finding out of an Achilles heel is frustrated by a consciousness that voluntarily bared it, before it
could be discovered. But I capitulate. If the most fruitless ob-

jection is still raised in the tenth year of my incorrigibility, any reply becomes useless. I simply cannot infuse into hearts made of parchment a feeling for the state of self-defense in which I live, for the special rights of a new form of writing and for the harmony between this seeming self-interest and the general goals of my work. They cannot understand that whoever totally identifies with some matter always talks to the point of that matter, and most of all when he talks about himself. They cannot understand that what they term vanity is actually that modesty which can never be quieted, which measures itself by its own standard, and that standard of mine is that humble striving for enhancement which always subjects itself to the most pitiless of judgments, which is always its own. Vain is the contentedness that never returns to the work. Vain is the woman who never looks into a mirror. Looking at oneself is essential for beauty and also for the mind. The world, however, has only one psychological noun for the two sexes and mistakes the vanity of a head finding inspiration and fulfillment in artistic creativity for the preening fussiness of working up a new coiffure. The world demands that one be responsible to it, not to oneself. The world considers it more important for someone not to regard his work as great than that it be great. The world wants an author's modesty; it would be prepared to overlook that of the achievement.

And in order once and for all to dispose of the idiocy that grows less modest every day, that resents my preoccupation with myself, my position, my books, and my enemies, and demonstrates admonishingly or derisively that this preoccupation takes up "half of my literary activity," when in fact it takes up all of my literary activity; and because this riffraff, for whom you can never be an authority as long as you are alive, will only leave you in peace if you cite "authorities;" in order to liquidate all the anonymous advisers and to complete the education of those worldly-wise nobodies who like to look things up in books, I welcome these words of Schopenhauer: "That one can be a great mind without noticing anything of it is an absurdity of which only hopeless incompetence can persuade itself, in order that it may regard the feeling of its own nothingness as modesty . . . I always have the suspicion about modest celebrities that they may well be right . . . Goethe has said it bluntly: 'Only good-for-nothings are modest.' But even more incontestable would be the assertion that those who so eagerly demand modesty from others, urge modesty, and unceasingly cry, 'Only be modest, for God's sake, only be modest!' *are assuredly good-for-nothings*, i.e., wretches entirely without merit, standard products of nature, ordinary members of the great pack of humanity."

TRANSLATED BY HELENE SCHER

The Cross of Honor

[1909]

In Austria there is a graduated scale of culpability for young
girls who embrace a life of vice. A distinction is made between
girls who are guilty of engaging in prostitution without authorization, girls who falsely declare that they are under the
supervision of the police morals division and, finally, girls
who are licensed to practice prostitution but not to wear a
cross of honor. This classification is confusing at first sight, yet
it is in complete accord with the facts of the situation.

A girl who looked suspicious to a detective (nothing looks
more suspicious to a detective than a girl) declared that she
was under the supervision of the police morals division. She
had only allowed herself the license of a joke, but the matter
was investigated. Since her declaration turned out to be false,
the police investigated her for unlawfully practicing prostitution. But when this suspicion also proved to be unfounded and
it turned out consequently that she was not practicing prostitution at all, the public prosecutor brought charges of mis-
representation against her. The girl had, so the accusation read,
"arrogated to herself in talking to a detective a social position

to which she was not entitled." She was practicing neither lawful nor unlawful prostitution and was therefore an imposter; and she escaped being sentenced only because during the hearing, in reply to the magistrate's question as to what had been in the back of her mind at the time, she replied, "Nothing."

To recapitulate: She had asserted that she was under the supervision of the police morals division. Because this was untrue, she was investigated by the police on suspicion of immoral conduct. She could prove all right that she was not immoral enough to lead an immoral life but, on the other hand, she could not prove that she was moral enough to be under the supervision of the police morals division. There was nothing left to do except charge her with making false statements, for which, after all, murderers are also sentenced in Austria in those cases where murder cannot be proved.

Now let us go a step further. It is possible that a girl who is licensed to practice prostitution might conceal the fact and fraudulently declare that she was not licensed to practice prostitution. She would then arrogate to herself an immoral life which she was not leading because she was licensed to do so but leading despite not being licensed to do so, being in fact licensed only to lead the immoral life for which she was licensed. Such cases rarely occur in practice, and the opinions of the Supreme Court vary considerably. But the most difficult case was one that recently occurred in Wiener-Neustadt. In a brothel in that suburb lives a girl who is licensed to practice prostitution, a girl who has never been in any trouble. She has never arrogated to herself an immoral life which she does not lead, and it has never been proved that she has falsely declared she does not practice any form of prostitution for which she is not licensed. But the devil pursued that hitherto unblemished girl, and one evening she walked about the salon of the house wearing a military cross of honor on her breast. "She thereby aroused in the guests . . ." well, what do you imagine she aroused in the guests? Not what you think, but the opposite: indignation. And when a daughter of joy arouses indignation in the guests of a house of joy, it is high time for the public prosecutor to step in.

In actual fact, the girl was charged with arousing an emotion for which she was not licensed. The first magistrate acquitted her. He said that the cross of honor was not an authorized military decoration and that the indignation aroused was merely the kind that the police could handle. To be sure, he thus acknowledged that the girl would have been guilty if she had worn, say, the order of Takowa. Now it is obvious that the unauthorized wearing of a military decoration might make a journalist culpable, but never a prostitute. In Wiener-Neustadt, however, the feminist movement seems to have made such strides that both sexes are considered equally capable of lusting after medals. At any rate, the lower court declared that a cross of honor does not constitute a military decoration.

The public prosecutor, however, was of a different opinion. He appealed, and the higher court imposed a fine of twenty crowns on the defendant. A cross of honor, the higher court held, was a badge of honor equivalent to any military decoration. And the court characterized "the wearing of a medal in a brothel" as a particularly aggravating circumstance. When the defendant was asked what had been in the back of her mind, she replied, "Nothing." But this time the answer availed her nothing. For a respectable girl could sooner presume to prostitution than a prostitute to a cross of honor. What excuse did she have? A civilian, she said, had given it to her as a gift: He was generous and had given her the cross of honor as her wages of shame. But then she should have slipped it into her stocking. Only the guests of a brothel are entitled to wear a cross of honor, and if they thereby incur the indignation of the girls, the girls would then be guilty of a culpable act. But if a guest gives a girl a cross of honor instead of twenty crowns, she may not wear the cross of honor, or else she must give twenty crowns to the court. For justice is a whore that will not be gypped and exacts the wages of shame even from the poor!

TRANSLATED BY FREDERICK UNGAR

Hans Müller in Schönbrunn

[1917]

Hans Müller, who did not have to go to the front in order to write letters from there—has recently looked death in the face. That is to say, he was in Schönbrunn, that is, in the zoo, and he described how the panther lay behind the bars looking at him. "I am alone in the cosmos," said Müller, who did not lose his presence of mind for one instant, until the time the article began to take shape in his head. To be sure, he had gone to Schönbrunn with the set plan of having some thought strike him concerning the panther from which comparisons with humanity might be drawn. The danger attracted him, but he had rather underestimated it. Contemplating the heroic situation now past, he put it in these simple words: "I am alone in the cosmos." We believe that he did indeed have this adventure, albeit just a short while ago he went so far as to claim to have been received by the German Emperor in the Vienna Hofburg. Here, however, Müller describes the panther, whose powerful impact he cannot shake off, down to its very nostrils "under which the bristles protrude, needle-fine."

He had not been to Schönbrunn for fifteen years. "In those

days the world was still wide and open . . . O multiplicity of
the world, captured like a drop of essence in the capsule of
memory . . ." he begins to muse, as only a Shakespearean king's
son or a Nestroyan shop clerk would muse after having seen one
of Müller's plays. These thoughts of Hans Müller's, which
sweep down to the Pampas and then make a side trip to Den-
mark, Sorrento, Spain, and the Vierwaldstättersee, appear to
bore the panther. For "the beast opens it jaws"—it yawns.
Müller misinterprets this, and believes he is now in that mortal
danger he thought he had been fortunate enough to escape by
posting his front-line column in Vienna and by his work in the
military archives.

This is a tense moment to which Müller does justice in the
brief but momentous sentence: "It then occurs that I advance
right up to the bars of the cage." Once assuming this occurrence to be true, we now wait for what is to occur next. "The
panther looks and does not move." What occurs at the same
time is that the panther, who until then had been no anti-
Semite, sees a gentleman from the *Neue Freie Presse** for the
first time. The panther waits, we wait. "His breath meets mine
in the still air," reports Müller, while we stay breathlessly in
the rear, all agog for what is to follow. "Our eyes grip into one
another." The panther, which certainly possessed a fine gift
for observation but no talent for description, would have portrayed this occurrence, which must have seemed just as significant to him, a little less impressionistically perhaps, but still
with dramatic force. But now, so says Müller, and the panther
does not contradict, "something monstrous, something which
cannot be put into words" (thank God) "as though from primeval creation, fills this uneventful moment." What had hap-

---

* The leading Viennese newspaper, which had a staff largely of
Jewish journalists and which was a Kraus target for many years.

pened? Could it really be? Did the panther—which at the sight of Hans Müller made a gesture meaning "Oy veh!" in the language of his species—intend to strike a decisive blow against the prestige of the *Neue Freie Presse*? No, the poor beast, feeling itself to be brilliantly observed, simply opened its jaws. It yawned, as we said. But Müller thought it wanted to devour him in order to prevent the article from being written.

Müller is fascinated. "As though enthralled, I gaze into this black gorge guarded by terrible, yellow, blade-sharp teeth." Müller understands that "the enmity between creature and creature will endure forever," for "on one and the same star there can never be neighborliness! To whom does the earth belong—?" The thinker snatched this pessimistic observation, which touches on one of those problems that can only be answered with another question, from the lion's jaws, so to speak, in a moment between life and death, which were separated only by a row of iron bars. "Now the panther draws its left forepaw from under its belly with a heavy movement, as though it were pregnant, and raised it." Something terrible is going to happen. "For a second he holds death upraised, the green glass of his eye becomes fluid." Run Müller! "For one second it is utterly quiet in the wilderness. Mortal foes." Will Müller attack? "Two beings whom no bridge can bring together stand and meet one another's gaze." Müller stands and hesitates. His mood is serious but confident. "Then—it is over." The panther is saved. It breathes a sigh of relief. Glad that there is no bridge that reaches from him to Müller, though Müller would have liked that.

"Wearily, the great cat draws its beautiful head back into its shoulders, its arm slides limply down the prison bars, and with a heavy, exhausted-sounding thud, its entire body drops to the cage floor." Overpowered by Müller's gaze. The panther feels rotten. (And how rotten.) What can a panther do against a

journalist? To whom does the earth belong? To the journalist!
Yet the victor is not haughty in his triumph. He will treat it mer-
cifully. "A sudden pity of the kind that cannot be explained
sends a tremor through me." He awards the lion's share of the
victory over the panther to the manager of the zoo who keeps
the panther locked up and has consequently removed any possibility of the free use of its powers.

"You poor slave"—Müller grows bitter—"have they robbed
you of your life?" Müller realizes that he has triumphed over a
defenseless opponent and wishes the panther were free. He
would like, if possible, to meet him in the primeval jungle. He
bewails the order of things which has brought it here, "here as
a spectacle for children." Only once in a blue moon, when a
man of letters turns up, does the panther know what its purpose
is on this earth. "Not with a single glance does the beast betray
that it is aware there is a person nearby. It lies there, senseless."
Poor wretch. Müller goes off and thinks about life, about the
world, about God.

Animals are not unprincipled journalists. They may well feel
the longing "for the common home of all living creatures,"—
that's how he interprets their nocturnal cries—but surely only
if that excludes war-scribblers who embrace the cosmos in
their off-duty hours. Hans Müller, as every baby elephant
knows, is the most successful author of the patriotic season,
and identical with that Hans Müller who publicly claimed to
have been received by the German Emperor in the Vienna Hofburg. Since, however, the German Emperor would not receive
a writer who had not been in the field, and most especially not
one who falsely claimed that he had, Hans Müller might no
more have been in the Hofburg than he was in the field. On the
other hand, it is entirely credible that he was in Schönbrunn.

TRANSLATED BY MARCUS BULLOCK

The Beaver Coat

[1919]

My life in Vienna has once again been enriched. There is an
end to slinking close to the house fronts to avoid being
spoken to on the sidewalk by some fool, and each day brings
new adventures. During all these years, no parties, no theater,
no parade of flower-decked carriages—how can anyone endure it? The supply of the most valuable impressions had been
cut off, and who knows how long one's inner resources would
have lasted? Even the season's catastrophes, the comet and
the hunting exhibition, seemed unable to alter anything in
this situation.

True—I make no secret of it—I expected to get some stimu-
lation out of the end of the world. But supposing that too
turned out to be just another flop? So one goes on existing from
day to day, along the same narrow path that always leads from
the same desk to the same restaurant, where one always eats
the same dishes and always avoids the same people. One does
not get to be any happier that way.

The world all around is colorful, and one would like to rub
up against it just to see if the color comes off. One doesn't

want to give up so much without finding out how little one is losing. Just one more time to sit at the abundant table, to hear again all the belches of the joy of living, to press the sweaty palm of brotherly love: such was my dream, and a good fairy—probably the one who sings their songs to operetta composers in the cradle—heard me. I am in the thick of it, the earth possesses me again*: my fur coat has been stolen.

Nothing could have brought me closer to my fellow men than the theft of my fur coat. Now it would take no less than the measures of a Caracalla to ward off their company. Now there is no way back to my retreat from life, now it's a matter of swallowing the bitter pill and being a friend to man. I have made myself hated long enough, but now they forgive me, they love me, they feel sorry for me, they admire me, for it can no longer be covered up, no denial will help—my fur coat has been stolen. And in an unguarded moment sociability had me by the collar.

I lived quietly and harmlessly. I was a private person, for I had been occupied with literary work for many years. I had not realized that above everything else I was the owner of a fur coat. I wrote books, but people understood only the fur coat. I offered myself as a sacrifice, and people thought of nothing but my fur coat. When I no longer possessed it, universal recognition ensued. By losing the fur coat, I justified the public's attention, which I had aroused by owning the fur coat. In the coffeehouse where it happened, the first reaction when the theft was discovered was a chaotic confusion, with several upset coffeehouse patrons forgetting to pay their checks. So suddenly was I thrust into the center of it that only by the roundabout route of reflection was I able to realize that it was definitely not *I* who had stolen the fur coat. People be-

---

* Part of a line from Goethe's *Faust*

haved as if they were about to tear from my body the clothes
I still had, and from all sides reproaches over my carelessness
descended upon me.

In this way indignation at the thief, who had eluded the
consequences of his actions, seemed to vent itself. For I was
still around, they could hold on to me, and when, exhausted
by the investigation of the case, I leaned back in the proper
frame of mind to read a newspaper at last, the chorus of my
fellow men went past me exclaiming, "What do you say to
that?" I felt the sting of reproach. Too late did I realize that if
one has a fur coat one also has certain obligations toward the
world at large, and I had no choice but to fulfill that final duty
to the world which one still has when one no longer has a fur
coat: the duty to render an accounting. For even when it becomes impossible to learn where the fur coat has gone, one
must at least inform the public and the police where it came
from, how much it cost, how much it is worth today, whether
the collar is long-haired or short-haired, and whether it has a
cloth or leather loop. The police furthermore inquire whether
one has any suspicions. A suspicion warms you when you no
longer have a fur coat, and in the view of the police, a suspicion you can hold on to is always sufficient compensation for
the certainty that has been lost and which they will never get
back for you.

Why this official meddling? I have always believed that the
police are concerned with public morality and not with matters of private life such as a stolen fur coat. But such curiosity!
No sooner had my coat been stolen than three representatives
of the police entered the premises, pushing their way through
the moneylenders who surrounded my table expressing their
outrage over the theft, and asked me if I had any suspicions.
Now the whole neighborhood was astir, for the rumor had
spread like wildfire through the city. Numerous passers-by

lingered at the official inquiry. Among them were personalities well known for their presence at premières and earthquakes. The discretion and dignity with which the theft of the fur coat was carried out were equaled by the blatancy and din with which the public expressed its sympathy. For fur thieves do not care to attract attention; bank robbers, on the other hand, place the highest value on being noticed everywhere and getting their names in the papers. Here, for once, they had miscalculated. Because the newspapers would take no notice even of a comet if its tail had grazed my head.

For the same reason I had to fear that the Chief of Police would not apply himself to this case as energetically as he commonly does when the prospect of journalistic support spurs him on to feverish activity. Of course, genuine professional interest does not let itself be turned aside by such considerations. While the representatives of authority questioned me about my age, occupation, and criminal record, some of the patrons repeatedly expressed their regret that they had not been looking just at the moment when the fur was taken, and they took the view that the thief must have chosen a moment when he felt unobserved. The staff were bombarded with questions, but the headwaiter, the waiter, the busboy, and the apprentice all shared just one desire: "Boy, if I could get my hands on a fellow like that just once, I'd sure beat his brains out!"

I begged them not to let themselves be carried away to the point of making dangerous threats in the presence of police detectives, but I also asked the latter to see to it that I would not have to appear in court, since I was unable to testify to more than that I had no fur coat and no suspicions, and I extricated myself from the ovations of the crowd, picked up my hat, which was still there, and headed for the exit, past the cashier, who was wringing her hands. Outside I was hailed by the carriage drivers who somehow or other were hoping for some special benefit from the day's event. One of the policemen, however, overtook me and proposed that I go with him and look through the rogues' gallery. I turned down this proposition, because I had no way of making a judgment as long as I had not seen the thief who had stolen my coat. Let the police produce him first; I would then be happy to make a formal identification from his photograph. But one of the waiters suddenly declared that he had a suspect in mind and seemed determined to come along. This investigation, as I later learned, did not essentially help my situation but yielded other gratifying results. The waiter, for one, is supposed to have recognized several former regular patrons of the café; and they say that never before had such a joyful atmosphere of reunion prevailed at a police station. Since there seemed to be no end to the outcries of "Jeez, Herr von Kohn!" and "Well, what do you know, Herr von Meier," the picture book finally had to be wrested from the good fellow's hands. The next day I received a summons, but I did not comply with it. Until now I had always managed scrupulously to avoid having anything stolen from me, for there is nothing I fear more than unpleasantness with the police. And, in fact, they have never been able to prove the slightest thing against me. Was I now, because of this one slip-up, to be saddled with such an embarrassing investigation? Never! I would not answer the summons! At least I was determined not to do so before they had recovered the fur coat. Besides, I hoped that they would hush the matter up and let me quietly pursue my accustomed occupation.

So, when I entered the café again and was about to go to the corner where I usually sat and read, I found several gentlemen there who normally were interested only in trotting races, but for this once had made a bet on whether or not I would recover

my fur coat. Those who were of the opinion that I would get
it back said, "No way he'll get it!" while the others who were
of the opinion that I would not get it back kept shouting, "Sure
he'll get it!" This way I could distinguish between the two
groups but was unable to come to a decision about the validity
of their predictions. I sat down and heard from the billiard
room shouts like: "Genuine beaver, I tell you!" "And I tell you,
mink!" at which a third voice plunged into the debate, saying
bluntly, "Astrakhan, you should have such luck!" I sent the
waiter to ask the gentlemen whether it would disturb them if
I read my newspapers. They answered in the negative and
changed to a different subject—one of them claimed he could
still remember the case of old man Loew's being robbed of a
coat worth about a thousand—imagine, a thousand—gulden;
and when someone else threw in the question, "Which Loew?"
he was given the reprimand, "Why, the one who went bankrupt later!"

I felt then that attention was diverted from me, and I was
glad of it. I picked up the newspaper that for years had been
known to interest the public by not mentioning my name and
searched for an item that would deal with the fact that a fur
coat had been stolen from a private individual, and that "a
member of our staff" had had the opportunity of speaking with
the thief, who was very widely known. At that point a lady I
did not know came up to me, scolded me on account of my
carelessness, and asked me whether I was still friendly with
the T—— family. I replied that I was not friendly with anyone at all, and paid my check. Outside, the carriage drivers
hailed me, gestured invitingly toward their vehicles, and then
shouted after me something like, "Don't you catch a cold, now!"

But I have not yet related what happened when I saw my
housekeeper the day after the deed. She was actually to blame,
for she had persuaded me—since we had just had a snowfall

in the severest May—to put on my fur coat, which during the winter had been kept in storage at the furrier's. I had balked at this, for some vague feeling told me that when there is a fresh snowfall the fur-coat thieves spring up out of the ground, while the people who shovel snow get no work because the municipality favors the competition of a spring thaw. Yet, although the thaw had already set in, the woman got her way; and sure enough, half an hour later the fur coat was stolen. Now, there is nothing more distressing to me than arguments about matters that have to do with the household; and consequently, after the misfortune had happened, the one concern I had was: How shall I tell my housekeeper? There was a lively scene, and I got to hear all sorts of things. For women's hearts are attached to worldly things, and only with great difficulty can they part even with other people's possessions; whereas I felt lighter when I was able to leave the café in the thaw without a fur coat.

On the whole, the loss of the fur coat had left me cold, and what really affected me was the loss of my peace and quiet. That I was the focus of attention, that overnight I had become a celebrity in Vienna, and that people were pointing their fingers at me with, "There he goes!" "Do you know him?" "But of course I do, beaver coat . . ." "He definitely didn't get it back"—that is what grieved me; that is what ate into me like moths into a fur coat that one has not been robbed of. I decided to avoid going out on the street until I heard grass grow over the matter. However, after a week, when I cautiously ventured into the restaurant I usually frequented and went in by the rear entrance, there, confronting me, was the woman who cleaned the restrooms, saying, "I sure was sorry!" When I entered the main room, all eyes were directed at me and my overcoat, and as I was hanging it up on the coatrack someone called out from one corner, "Now you've got to be twice as

careful!" And from the other corner, "Once bitten, twice shy."
When a waiter intervened, saying, "But the gentleman is careful anyway," a voice shouted frcm the game room, "A burnt
child dreads the fire." The waiter said, "If I could just get my
hands on him once, I'd. . . ."

I paid my check immediately and made up my mind to come
to the restaurant only at night, when a different crowd of people would be there. But no sooner had I taken a seat under
such altered circumstances than an English horse trainer turned
around to me, pushed his chair forward, and with his arms
propped on the arm rest began in halting German, "Once a
horse blanket was stolen of me. . . ." I saw that in addition to
filling the Viennese population's need to communicate, my
experience was meeting with international interest. I feared
that here there could be the beginning of an increase in tourist
traffic. I locked myself in and did not show myself until hot
weather seemed to burn out every association with the idea of
a fur coat. But then I had to experience having a Negro come
up to me who spoke German so perfectly that he was able to
ask me whether I had recovered my fur coat that time. I sought
out a different restaurant, the proprietor of which not only
molested me by his greeting but also by addressing me with
the words: "That won't happen to you at our place."

I realized that there was no way back for me any longer. For
here a Viennese problem had been born. Here there was just
the kind of incident, so plausible in its fascination, and with
such immediate popular appeal, that no consideration for the
person affected could keep people at a distance. Here a solidarity was established through the realization, amazing in its sim-
plicity, that this could happen to any of us. I was drawn into the
circle of a community that kept guard for me over my stolen
fur coat, a community that with its glances seemed to be taking
my measurements for a new coat without making me a present

of one. All that was lacking now was to have the Tax Office become interested in the case, and it could indeed easily have found out that I am in the financial circumstances that allowed me to have owned a fur coat. I began to envy the thief—not because he had the fur coat, but because he had not been found out. Because he could move freely, whereas behind me people cried "Stop, thief!" and I, like someone caught red-handed in the act of being robbed, was escorted by stupidity. . . . I decided to retire from private life. I had one hope left: that through the publication of a new book I would succeed in making the Viennese forget my existence.

TRANSLATED BY SHEEMA Z. BUEHNE

Bread and Lies

[1919]

"It is therefore indispensable for the reconstruction of the world to strengthen the very backbone of life—imagination. This could be effected only through the elimination of need and, consequently, the liberation of the human spirit from concern with it, together with checking the flow from the false well-springs of an alienated life. For in proportion to the spirit's exposure to the necessities of life, its desire grew to see the imagination replaced by something external, and the more this replacement was perfected, the more did the end become the victim of the means.

"Only a policy that acknowledges man as the goal and life as the means is viable. That other policy, which reduces man to the means, cannot foster life either and must militate against it. That policy all the more eliminates that heightened form of humanity, the artist, while a normal, matter-of-fact order of things at least allows him the space willed by nature. That policy admits a purely aesthetic relationship between the individual and the created work, for it endorses the product of the creative act merely as an ornament and a deceitful veneer of an ugly life. It does not even appreciate the importance of the work itself, affirming instead only the right of the privileged to enjoy the work, whose creator altogther vanishes behind the questionable Maecenas of a materialistically oriented society. It breeds snobbery, which is hostile to all that is original, and therefore opposed to all that is creative, and which believes its relationship to art legitimated, if it places the protection of already existing works of art above the concern for life's needs. Yet the meaning of art is fulfilled only when the meaning of life itself is not in the decline, and symphonies come into being only if adjacent life, wounded to death, does not groan for mercy. In reality, however, the mystery out of which every work of art is wrung, contains that mystic harmony with all living creatures, the impoverishment of which inevitably impoverishes the creative soul. For while material abundance can live alongside distress, benefiting from it, the man of divine creativity cannot—he suffers with it in sympathy, wasting away from this simultaneity with an unfulfilled life, and drying up from the sinful contrast between plenty and want with which every age confronts the conscience and responsibility of the man of a nobler nature.

"In a culture that purchases luxury with human sacrifice, art leads a merely decorative life. A people's creative powers, like all its vital virtues, are inhibited by splendor and by misery equally, and most of all by the woeful curse of their combination. The power to give, like the right to receive, is contingent upon the assurance that life exist neither below its needs nor above them, that it be sacrificed neither to want nor luxury but be nurtured for its own sake and for the joyous experience of communion with all of nature, as "the share in this life," an experience which God intended for the spider no less than for a Goethe.

"Man, however, has wilfully foregone this sharing and has

forfeited his very self. And from this age, which dishonors God's creatures and binds the meaning of life with the chains and fetters of material concern, every grace of creation has fled. If the God-given right to receive beauty is diminished, the ability to bestow it languishes too. There is room remaining only for that unholy talent which masters also the hostile reality of this age and is stirred by its dissonances. The consequence is—despite my clearest awareness of the problematic character of my own writings—the more or less total nonexistence of a contemporary literature in the German language.

"I do not know how matters stand in painting, an art form in which creations do not survive their material elements. I do know, however, that if painting involves, like language, an interdependence with all living things, it too can produce a Rembrandt only if death does not dominate creation all around. I also know that in a time of desolation the truly creative act would be the resolve to cover a freezing man's nakedness with the canvas of the available Rembrandt. For the spirit stands higher than man, it is true, but higher than the creations of the spirit stands man—and he can be a Rembrandt."

I wrote these words in July 1919, at a time when the word hunger had long been a newspaper item to the wealthy of this city but had not yet begun to spill over into the theater and art news. I do believe that for hearts still capable of harboring living thoughts a harmony could be perceived here between basic human concerns between the meaning of life and the conception of art, as an undreamed-of bond by which life and creativity appear to be integrated in a freer world like a discovery of their poles: the individual and the community and yet their common function of encompassing one and the same world.

But an author's thoughts seldom are the reasons for his readers to have any of their own. Where receptive hearts are lacking, comprehending heads are wanting too. How minimally matters of the spirit are likely to have an impact on their times and provide a means for immediate comprehension, is demonstrated in exemplary fashion by my own fate—that of a profound ineffectiveness, which owes even its popularity to misunderstanding. I therefore feel fairly well qualified to express my views on the total superfluity of all art treasures.

If spiritual forces possessed that gift of persuasion which adheres to mere opinions, then in twenty years that great evil to which we owe the destruction of so many of this world's values and hopes would have been stamped out. I mean the press, which has brought about endless terror and is now bringing about a terrifying end, not through the dissemination of dangerous views but through the deadly power of its very presence, which is hostile to the spirit.

Moving from the insignificant example of my own writing to those cultural possessions so dear to the hearts of the guardians of the temple of art, I could ask whether those arch-liars, who most certainly gauge value by effect, honestly believe that the possessions in front of which they extend their protecting arms, lest, God forbid, our hunger be reduced by a few weeks, are really more valuable than the foreign currency with which we might buy grain. Do they really believe that these possessions are more valuable, if all their magic did not prevent us from getting into this predicament, and if all those edifying objects so indispensable to culture did not prevent us from amusing ourselves for a time with mustard-gas grenades and flame throwers? And that, as a consequence of this, we are worth these treasures only for our bodily survival but that we are no longer worthy of them; and that our ultimate defeat is not that we now have a right only to food but that we do not now have a right to the happiness of salvaging from the war a culture that was not sufficiently part of ourselves to keep us from engaging in that war.

Only too gladly do I leave it to the art experts to decide

whether tapestries have any place in the temple in which our bloodsuckers and profiteers perform their devotions before Rembrandt and Dürer. As one in whose soul, through all his life, only the color of nature found admittance, I trust blindly in the traditional belief that paintings constitute part of that inalienable spiritual heritage of humanity without which we could not imagine life itself, far less visualize ourselves at our present sublime stage of development.

I cannot divine the mystery that inspires the genius to create his world out of finite materials destined to ruin and suppose that that timeless impact, without which art would be no more than a vulgar pastime or ornament, must be inherent in the act of creation itself. Now, since I know as little about the conditions under which these works are produced as about the mysteries of their conception, my ignorance may be suspected of being the fundamental antipathy of the color-blind, were it preeminently on works of fine art that I manifest my unshakeable belief that life is more important than works of art. My answer to the question as to whether works of art ought to be exchanged for food I have unambiguously anticipated with my advice about covering the nakedness of a freezing man with even the most valuable canvas.

This example—distasteful aesthetically and to which rationality objects because of the impracticableness of the brittle fabric—suggesting itself as the decision between ultimate values in the realm of need, i.e., between still life and still breathing life, illustrates the thought that humanity faced with its most primary problem must renounce creativity and the enjoyment of what was created. The spirit, when true to itself, turns from the aesthetic to the ethical and so to compassion.

There can be altogether no doubt that I shall regard rights of ownership as no obstacle when it is a question not of destroying a work of art to protect a person from freezing but only of changing its location as a protection against starvation. Since,

however, there are supposed to be considerations even weight-
ier than those of ownership forbidding the sale of works of art,
and since even the vilest lie of which in all our misery, we
are still capable, namely, our culture forbids this, it is time
that I abandoned a field in which I cause a stir only through
my ignorance, turned to that area in which not even my
deadliest enemy would deny me a certain amateur's relationship, and focused my attention on a cultural danger, which
does not yet threaten us but which even in times of plenty I
would wish may be inflicted upon us.

The profoundest objection to the sale of tapestries, and
one recurring in all the protests, is the observation that bread,
once it has been eaten, is no longer there, while in art we possess something durable. On the assumption that the government, in deciding upon the method of first satisfying hunger
with bread and in the meantime trusting in God or some other
help, failed to consider what a wise man called their attention
to, namely, the transitoriness of food in contrast to the intransi-
toriness of tapestries; and should the government be of the
opinion that we can live from the "bacon that will last only for
a few weeks," in the future also, then let the following sugges-
tion be offered to it: not to forget, once the museums are
empty, that there are also libraries to stave off hunger.

And with that I have reached the point at which my cultural
nihilism does merit some confidence and where I am on account of my profession entitled to prefer destruction to the
misuse of lying. Now, when it comes to selling books, I well
know that the multiple availability of one and the same literary
work as well as the fact that its comprehension is limited by
national language factors are considerations that reduce to almost nothing the sales value in comparison to the sums to be
derived from the sales of works of art; nevertheless the bib-
liophilic factor would in countless instances prove its appeal.

To illustrate the urgency of saving naked life, I have preferred the example of painting only because canvas offers a more likely protection against cold than paper, which serves this beneficent end only when it is combusted. Yet I will not permit the suspicion to arise that, in order to work on a cold night, I would not be prepared to use my own works for fuel, if I had ever had the desire to own them. The certainty of the dead value of all cultural possessions—and how much more dead they are in the hands of these contemporaries—has always restrained me from striving after a success that is foreign to all authentic artistic production.

And if indeed I am to be believed—however few may know or feel it—that I would not let any material impediment stand in my way to the perfecting of a word, its justification to me, that is, its standing the test before the forum most authoritative for me, and then, still without reassurance, beyond this forum on to an imagined high court of language; and if I am to be believed that for the sake of a comma I would not spare myself a journey to the most distant printing plant and even then return unsatisfied—then even he who most basely misjudges my evaluation of my finished (only seemingly finished) work which, whether or not I could complete it, has caused me endless doubt and whose final completion endless regret—even he will discover in it every other desire than that for applause.

If I did not also derive from the public recitation of my writings the satisfaction befitting my self-conscious claim to the enjoyment of acting, it would be only the anguish of the author who has never cast a glance at his printed works except to alter them cheerfully for subsequent editions and who at the recitation table must helplessly suffer them in all their imperfection and, even while gratifying his ear, makes mental notes for later corrections.

The erroneous supposition that the soul that harbors such

intangible concerns might contain room for success must surely be refuted by the observation that it has after all been able to endure the monstrous and daily experienced void all these years. The error sustains itself on the misunderstanding of that historical obligation that I have laid upon myself together with my other higher duties: namely, to acknowledge in my own writings signals of my existence in other people's publications and to collect, with still greater pride and satisfaction, all those moments in which the practice of silence about me is proved.

What more flagrant infamy than its attitude toward me could I uncover in the official literary world? In what other instance could I make more obvious its wretched sham, the exposure of which I consider my duty? And what, apart from its own complicity in our shameful war, could better reveal the vicious lying of this feuilletonism of ours than the thievish dexterity with which it acclaims, as intellectual achievements, pronouncements I made in 1914, while attributing them to those who by 1918 were already bold enough to steal them from me?

If only those uncomprehending individuals who reproach an author for his self-esteem would finally recognize that it prevails only up until the time that a book goes to press—and up to then, to be sure, prevails to an unimaginable, indeed boundless, degree—but after that emerges only as renunciation of a success-oriented world! And I really believe that none of the creators with whom the man of culture boasts familiarity, creators who, were it not for the dubious medium of literary history, would most certainly not be known to the present generation, has ever regarded his work differently, with less vanity or less modesty.

By absolutely not sparing my own writings in the utilization of my library for fuel, I protect my general disrespect for works already created against the suspicion that I am out to strike willfully at works other than books and that I aim at the impoverishment of art galleries. And, turning to the object of the verbal art, it is the writer who will best be able to convey to a war-torn world expiring in the midst of works of beauty, the conviction that, in the name of art and of all eternal life, man stands above the created work.

To state my demands with all necessary inexorability, let us suppose that the intention were not, as with works of fine art, merely a relocation, through which nothing more than the conditions affecting their immediate impact would be changed (perhaps even for the better)—but rather the destruction of our literary treasures, even the totality of all books wherever they are—a catastrophe one could more readily imagine inflicted through an accident of war's purposelessness rather than through the politics of coal shortages.

Thus I maintain with the persistence that has brought me so little success that one newspaper has done more to hamper our moral development than the complete works of Goethe have done to foster it! For this reason I anticipate some gain from the systematic destruction of all existing newsprint (after wars that mankind owes to the newspapers) but fear no loss from the accidental destruction of all literary works—through wars waged by mankind in spite of them.

That is my conviction, and as testimony I cite the fact that the Germans, however much they may lie, are very vocal about their culture—and that in a hundred years they have not been so proud of their Goethe as in five years of their bombers. I believe that an investigation as to how many Germans have read Goethe's *Pandora* and how many have read Richthofen's *Roter Kampflieger* (Red Fighter Pilot) would produce a result that would not exactly justify our arrogance in cultural affairs. Nor let anyone object that war is war. If Goethe's countrymen had not lied in peacetime, they would have admitted that they considered Geibel a far greater poet than Goethe.

And what could better prove the superfluity of timeless values to the German soul than the circumstance that it was only last year that Cotta's publishing house sold the last of one thousand copies of the first edition of Goethe's *West-östlicher Divan*? What danger to a literary shrine does it require to stir up German cultural consciousness? Every art bluffer would like to save our consciences from the disgrace of selling a picture abroad, when there was no disgrace attached to buying it and bringing it here in the first place. What worse disgrace threatens the hunting tapestry than that it will hang in Paris instead of Vienna?

The self-forgetfulness that causes the German guardian of culture to make his protests becomes most clearly evident in the fact that none of them, even for a moment, is frightened by the possibility that he himself could be adduced as proof that in Germany there is no culture endangered.

From the belief in the deeper indispensability and inalienability of art to the shallow delusion that we cannot manage without the object and without touching the object, is about as far as from my desk to a protest rally at which art philistines get excited, when a work of art is threatened about which they know less than the bacon to which they think themselves superior, so long as they have it. As long as what was to them a matter of course does not become a problem, and the only problem, and so does not touch their own, their physical life.

It gives me a pleasure that I can hardly express in words to put myself protectively in front of groceries if the government should dare want to sell them in exchange for the ideals of the Vienna Artists Association. What is left for one like me but to think of butter when they start raving about the exalted celestial goddess?

But what is left to those who are not so cosmopolitan but are rather more parochial? Why should we, through our tapestries, help France obtain immortality? Once, it is true, we were also concerned for her immortality. We are reminded of those days when we still had enough to eat but no longer enjoyed the food because the *Mona Lisa* had been stolen from the Parisians. It was the sign of the cultural solidarity that then spanned Europe that we all, including also that overwhelming majority that had never seen her and had up to then taken her for a Parisian stripteaser—that we all felt her disappearance as the most severe encroachment on our spiritual possessions.

For Vienna's artistic conscience does not react so intensely to the additions of a museum as it is wounded by the losses it suffers. It is of such nature that it would be far less pleased by the recovery of the *Mona Lisa* than wounded by its disappearance. Its sensitivity on this point goes so far that exactly those are most violently moved by the loss of an art treasure who only learn of its existence when it is lost and who know of the Museum of Art no more than that it is the opposite of the Museum of Natural History.

No, the intellectual does not learn any way other than by the immediate experience that affects him personally and physically. Object lessons of naked need, such as he could have a hundredfold every hour, do not suffice to move his heart.

It is just this that is most difficult to comprehend for people who believe that the peace has ended the war. The only attestation of a sick age is the slogan: Now the war is over! They solemnly deny that there was a war. They have had their fill of it. People of this type who, through four years, did not wish to realize they had started the war, now do not wish to accept the fact that they have lost it; they even act as if they had never waged this war.

An experience that through all the misery of this war and what it left behind should spread euphoria for a millennium— no longer to have Hapsburgs and Hohenzollerns—this gift of

fate is squandered on the recollection that under the mon-
archies smoked pork loin cost two Kronen, which then were
still one Mark and a half; the successor is the one blamed for
the higher cost of living.

The spiritual sapping of the war years has rendered us incapable of grasping the simple thought that the emperor is to
be blamed for this condition. And the patient whose leg must
be amputated so that his life may be saved is also wounded
psychologically to such an extent that he blames the doctor for
his suffering and calls for his mortal enemy, who, it is true, had
shot him but who would never have demanded that the patient
have his leg amputated. And because the fire brigade had to
destroy this and that, the victim holds it responsible not only
for the water but also for the fire itself, and, in order to be res-
cued, wishes for the arsonist.

Now I must say that, if the return of the evil were so surely
to guarantee all conceivable relief and indemnification as its
regime has brought about all profiteering and devastation, I
would still prefer to starve and freeze to death in the republic.
But those who have led us into the abyss have disappeared too
soon. As the unmistakable exponents of misery, they should
have accompanied us yet a while down to the bottom-most
depths, so that a world made more stupid through its suffering might pass away without longing for them and without a
desire to experience them once more.

For the most disastrous legacy the dynasts have left us is
not misery but the curse of a mental state in which we have
become incapable of perceiving our delivery from them as the
real gain of our suffering, incapable of valuing this gain as the
true meaning of that suffering, and have become unworthy of
being rid of them.

Through the way they waged war, we have not only been
set back in civilization by centuries; in our mental state we

have arrived where we have never been before. Merely by having been so highly fit for war we are unfit for a freedom whose gigantic magnitude does not correspond to an inner call. Nothing is left to us but the press, which will survive us, nothing but the lie to which we are accustomed and which no revolution will tear out of our souls. He who has not died of it, continues lying. For in order to live, he needs the lie as others do a bite of bread.

TRANSLATED BY EDWARD MORNIN
AND FREDERICK UNGAR

COMMENTS

A Minor Detail

[1915]

I am looking for a
Father-in-Law
to join me in establishing
a dress business. I am 35,
with wholesale and retail experience.
No middlemen. J. C.
Box No. 3378, Berlin SW.*

Cherchez la femme does not seem the appropriate phrase here.
Look for the little woman! Where can she be? He does not seek
to "marry into" the business, for he, the father-in-law, has not
yet set himself up in business. At least they used to say that
they wanted to find the business and were therefore looking for
the wife. After all, they needed a living pretext. This has now
fallen by the wayside; the father-in-law is the vestige of a
superseded stage of development, one that still indulged in

---

* An advertisement in a local newspaper.

sentimentality and included the wife in the stock of merchandise. That's all over.

Now it is a father-in-law who is being advertised for. The daughter can be dead if she likes. If she is present at the wedding, fine; if not—not. Will he share the marriage bed and the merchandise with his father-in-law? It is an innovation in the ladies' garment trade. Garments without ladies. The radiance of classical grandeur illumines our era. Where is she, the girl this fate will befall, the girl who may be reading the personal ad and does not know that in the end it actually concerns her. Where does the piece of merchandise live? Where does this ready-made garment of a woman live? Where is she, that I may entreat her to hide and kill herself sooner than become the cadaver for this hyena? Men now die by accident, women will bear children, because two men want to go into business.

A heroic age is dawning. Do not lament the past. Welcome, sunrise! In these great times two scoundrels will shake hands over the dead life of a girl.

TRANSLATED BY SHEEMA Z. BUEHNE

War-Weary

[1917]

War-weary is the stupidest phrase of this time. To be war-weary means to be weary of murder, weary of robbery, weary of lies, weary of hunger, weary of sickness, weary of dirt, weary of chaos. Was one ever fresh and unweary of all that? Then to be war-weary is truly a condition that does not merit saving. You ought always to be war-weary, not after but before the war has started. Because of war-weariness, wars should not be ended but refrained from. Nations in the fourth year of waging war that are war-weary deserve no better than continuing to suffer.

[The two selections below were delivered by Kraus at a public reading in Berlin on May 8, 1917. Wilhelm's actual speech was delivered by the Kaiser to his troops shortly before that date. It took no little courage for Kraus to repeat the speech and to contrast it with a quotation from Kant's *Toward Perpetual Peace* in reply.—*Editor's note*]

A Kantian and Kant

Kaiser Wilhelm II

The year 1917, with its great battles, has demonstrated that the German people have an absolutely reliable ally in the Lord of the Heavenly Host on high. On Him we can rely as surely as on our cannon; without Him we could not have done it. Only yesterday I saw and talked to your comrades near Verdun, and it was like a scent of morning air breezing through our souls. . . . We don't know what still lies ahead of us. But you have all seen how in these last four years God's hand has visibly ruled, has punished treason and rewarded brave perseverance, and from this we can take confidence that henceforth the Lord of the Heavenly Hosts will also be with us. If the enemy does not want peace, then we must bring peace to the world by smashing, with iron fist and glittering sword, the doors of those who do not want peace.

The total victory in the east fills me with profound gratitude. It allows us to experience one of the great moments in which we can reverently admire the hand of God in history. What a decisive turn by God's dispensation! The heroic deeds of our

troops, the successes of our great generals, the admirable
achievements of the home front have their roots, in the last
analysis, in the moral powers, in the categorical imperative in
which our people, in hard schooling, have been educated. . . .

All the more gratefully is God's judgment felt in eastern
Prussia in particular. Not least do we owe our victory to the
moral and spiritual powers that the great sage of Königsberg
[Kant] has given our people. . . . May God help us further to
ultimate victory!

Immanuel Kant

After the end of a war, at the conclusion of peace, it may not
be unseemly that, after a festival of thanksgiving, a day of
penance be proclaimed to invoke mercy in the name of the
state for the great sin the human race still commits in being
unwilling to submit to legal covenants in its relationship to
other peoples; proud of its independence, it prefers rather to
use the barbaric means of war by which what is sought—the
rights of all states—is not achieved.

The festivals of thanksgiving during the war for a victory
won, the hymns sung to the Lord of the Heavenly Hosts conflict no less with the moral idea of a Father of all men because,
aside from indifference to the way nations seek their mutual
rights (which is sad enough), they add the joy of depriving so
many people of their happiness.

A Change of Heart

[1919]

I

Berlin, May 31, 1918

Mr. Karl Kraus
Publisher of *Die Fackel*
Vienna

For twelve years I have been one of your admirers and only
recently, when you gave a public reading here, I presented you
with a little token* of my esteem.

But I cannot deny that I have been repelled by the way you
have abused my country during the war and that I disassoci-
ated myself from you. Again and again your genius attracted
me, but now I can no longer go along with you. Life in Germany and Austria is hell, you say. We alone started the war, we
alone continue it, everything evil is on our side, all glory and
all right are on the other side. This is the impression one gets
when one reads *Die Fackel.*

I shall continue to admire you and at the same time fight you

* A rare book on Jean Paul.

to the best of my ability. After my last letter to you I find it necessary to let you know this.

(signature)

II

Berlin, December 10, 1918

Dear Sir:

I wholeheartedly apologize for my last letter. For ten [sic] years I was your follower and departed from this path only when I believed you were sinning against my country. But you alone were right; in everything. I have no other excuse but that I was ensnared in a net of lies. Thus I have to ask your forgiveness.

Yours,
(signature)

That all glory and all right were on the other side could hardly be deduced from any of my war writings, but instead the ethical commandment to recognize and confess the shabbiness and the wrong on one's own side. If those of some influence on the other side do their duty, mankind will be helped; we have to do ours. This duty is not fulfilled with the coming of peace. The enemy must forget what his enemy has done to him and must never forget what he has done to his enemy. Both, unfortunately, are sinning against both these commandments.

TRANSLATED BY FREDERICK UNGAR

[The following advertisement appeared in 1920 in the journal of the German authors' guild. It was reproduced in its entirety the same year in *Die Fackel.—Editor's note*]

Who will write a

Book of Hatred

directed against the French hereditary enemy

based on historical facts, which sets the recent infamous deeds of the inferior "victor" in their proper light and summons our people to unite against the enemy? The book should be used—perhaps even primarily used—as a text for juveniles. Material can be supplied by the publisher.

So that this advertisement could appear in the journals of the *Allgemeiner deutscher Schriftstellerverband* (General German Authors Guild) and the *Kartell lyrischer Autoren* (Association of Lyric Poets), ten million people had to die with twice that number crippled and a hundred million become beggars. Would it not be inhuman to answer such hatred with humaneness and not consent to have such a writers' guild extradited to the victors bag and baggage?

I have imposed on myself a duty toward another age, which will be less ambiguously minded toward me, by compiling the spiritual inventory that it must know in order to reject its heritage, thus assuring that a chronicle exists of this wicked banality! Because the only record that will be of value for this age is the documentary evidence that will summon it before posterity.

TRANSLATED BY FREDERICK UNGAR

Tourist Trips to Hell

[1920]

I have in my hands a document* that surpasses and seals the shame of this age, and would warrant assigning a place of honor in a cosmic boneyard to this money-hungry mess that calls itself mankind. If ever a newspaper clipping meant a clipping of creation—here we face the utter certainty that a generation to which such solicitations could be directed no longer has any better instincts to be violated.

After the enormous collapse of the pretense of culture, and after the nations have proved by their actions that their relationship to anything in the realm of the spirit is of the most shameless deception—perhaps good enough to further the tourist trade but never sufficient to raise the moral level of this mankind—nothing is left but the naked truth of mankind's condition, which has almost reached a point where it is no longer able to lie. In no portrait could it recognize itself as well as in this one.

---

* An advertisement in the Basel (Switzerland) newspaper *Basler Nachrichten*, the bulk of which is quoted on the following pages.

BATTLEFIELD EXCURSION

Arranged by the
Basler Nachrichten

**Tourist trips
from September 25
to October 25
at the reduced price
of 117 francs**

Unforgettable impressions

No passport necessary

*To register
just fill out
the questionnaire.*

*Especially recommended
as a Fall trip!*

". . . the trip through the battlefield of Verdun conveys to the visitor the quintessence of the horror of modern warfare. It is not only the French who consider this a battlefield par excellence, on which the gigantic struggle between France and Germany was ultimately decided. No other battlefield of the West will make as deep an impression on anyone who sees this part of the front, with Fort Vaux and Fort Douamont in the center. If the entire war cost France 1,400,000 dead, almost one third of them were killed in that sector of Verdun comprising a few square kilometers, and the German losses were more than double. In that small sector, where perhaps more than 1,500,000 bled to death, there is no square centimeter not rutted by shells. Afterward one drives through the area of the Argonne and Somme battles, walks through the ruins of Reims, and returns via St. Mihiel and through the Priester Woods; all this is only a mere run-through of details which, at Verdun, combine to create an unbelievably impressive picture of horror and frightfulness . . ."

Everyone who inquires receives a printed guide listing the detailed itinerary for the trip and all necessary information. Trips depart every day. Comfortable seating is guaranteed to every participant.

TRIPS BY CAR!

600 kilometers by rail, second class. An entire day through the battlefields in a comfortable car, overnight stay, first-class meals, wine, coffee, tips, passport formalities and visas from Basel round trip, all included in the price of 117 Swiss francs.

- You leave Basel in the evening in an express train, second class.
- You are picked up at the Metz railway station and taken by car to the hotel.
- You stay overnight at a first-class hotel, service and tips included.
- You receive an ample breakfast in the morning.
- You leave Metz in a comfortable car and ride through the battlefield area of 1870–71 (Gravelotte).
- You have a guided tour of the highly interesting blockhouse in Etain (quarters of the Crown Prince and site of a large German headquarters).
- You ride through the destroyed villages in the fortress area of Vaux with its gigantic cemeteries holding hundreds of thousands of dead.
- You inspect, with a guide, the subterranean casemates of Fort Vaux.
- You visit the Ossuaire (boneyards) of Thiamont where the remains of the unidentified dead are constantly deposited.
- You drive along the Ravin de la Mort past the Carrières d'Haudromont at the foot of the Côte du Poivre to Verdun.
- You have lunch in the best hotel in Verdun, with wine and coffee, tips included.
- You have time after lunch to visit destroyed Verdun and Ville Martyre, and passing through the battlefields of 1870–71 you return to Gravelotte and Metz.
- You have dinner in your hotel in Metz with wine and coffee, tips included.
- You are taken to the station by car after dinner.
- You return to Basel on a night express second class.

Everything included in the price of 117 francs, with ample meals at first-rate restaurants

A large number of letters of praise and appreciation from people who have taken the trip is available at our office.

But what does it mean, this picture of horror and frightfulness revealed by one day at Verdun—what does it mean, this most gruesome spectacle of bloody delirium through which the nations let themselves be dragged to no purpose whatsoever, compared with the enormity of this ad! Is the mission of the press not revealed here—first to lead mankind to the battlefields, and then the survivors?

- You receive a newspaper in the morning.
- You will read how comfortable survival is made for you.
- You will learn that 1,500,000 bled to death exactly at the spot where wine and coffee—and everything else—are included.
- You have the decided advantage over the martyrs and the dead of first-class meals in Ville Martyre and at the Ravin de la Mort.
- You ride to the battlefield in a comfortable car, but they got there only in cattle cars.
- You learn about all that is offered as compensation to you for their sufferings and for an experience whose purpose, sense, and cause you have been unable to grasp to this day.
- You understand that all this came about so that some day, when nothing was left of the glory except moral bankruptcy, at least a battlefield par excellence would still be available.
- You learn that there is still something new at the

battlefront, and that one can live better there now than before on the home front.

- You realize that what the competition can offer—the Argonne and Somme battles, the boneyards of Rheims and St. Mihiel—is a mere trifle compared with the first-class offering of the *Basler Nachrichten*. They will doubtless succeed to fatten their list of subscribers using the casualties of Verdun.
- You understand that the goal is to make the tourist trip pay, and the tourist trip was worth the World War.
- You receive an ample breakfast, even if Russia starves to death, as soon as you make up your mind to take in the battlefields of 1870–71 as well—all in one package.
- You still have time after lunch to see the remains of the unidentified dead brought in, and after completion of this program event you still have an appetite for dinner.
- You learn that the nations whose victim you are in war and in peace will even spare you passport formalities —no minor matter—if the trip goes to the battlefield and if you get your ticket through the newspaper by the deadline.
- You realize that these nations have criminal laws to protect the life and even the honor of these press scoundrels who make a mockery of death and a profit out of catastrophe, and who particularly recommend this side trip to hell as an autumn special.
- You will have difficulty not violating these laws, but afterward you will be expected to send a letter of appreciation and thanks to the *Basler Nachrichten*.
- You will have unforgettable impressions of a world in which there is no single square centimeter not rutted by shells and advertisements.
- And if, even then, you have not recognized that your

very birth has brought you into a murderers' pit and that a mankind which profanes even the blood it shed is shot through and through with evil, and that there is no escaping it and no help—then the devil take you to a battlefield par excellence!

LETTERS

Joseph Schöffel

Died February 7, 1910
in the 78th year of his life

[1 9 1 0]

"Lock up your hearts more carefully than your gates.
The days of betrayal are coming; and it has been given
free rein."

GOETHE

The *Neue Freie Presse* did not say when he was to be buried.
It described the course of his life with calm objectivity. It did
not pay its respects to the dead but simply threw a handful of
words over him.

"At the beginning of the seventies he stepped to the fore
publicly when the plan of cutting down the Vienna Woods sur-
faced. At that time Schöffel successfully championed the preservation of the Woods."

This sentence is all that is said about a deed for which one
hundred and four municipalities made the man an honorary
citizen, a deed in honor of which memorials were erected during his lifetime. The *Neue Freie Presse* is stingy with words,
the old whore. She is wicked. The manliest man in Austria
never frequented her. The fact that he lived is something she
cannot forgive him even in death. But I do not want her to forget his voice. I want to have him speak to her and tell her what
he spoke into my phonograph in 1901.

Dear Sir:

Many thanks for so kindly sending me your journal *Die Fackel* which, by the way, I have been reading ever since its first appearance. I feel with you in your battle against the terroristic, shameless dealings of today's pirates of the press, and I wish you the utmost success! Unfortunately, you, as I, alone and forsaken, are confronting an exceedingly powerful opponent who is without conscience and without honor in his choice of means and methods.

I am an old man whose last ounce of strength is being absorbed by his duties in public office. Nothing would otherwise prevent me from coming to your side and acting as your second in your battle—as my unforgettable friend Ferdinand Kürnberger* once did in my battle for the Vienna Woods.

Today, if Kürnberger could hear that the *Neue Freie Presse*, this monstrosity of August Zang's—Kürnberger, who, in 1873 described that newspaper as a government-licensed procuress, a procuress of every kind of corruption, the most insolent mistress of all crooks who swindle the government—if today, thirty years after the conclusion of the battle for the Vienna Woods, he could hear that the *Neue Freie Presse* was posing as protector of those very same Woods that no one is threatening, he would blast away the mound of earth beneath which he sleeps in order to strike this shameless prostitute in the face. The *Neue Freie Presse* as protector of the Vienna Woods, she who set in motion the selling-off of government-owned property, who favored the contract with Moriz Hirschl for logging the forest and countenanced the sale of the Vienna Woods as a financial necessity, who, when the storm began, at first passed over my battle in dead silence, then mocked me, and declared that I was

* Writer and liberal journalist (1821–1879).

stricken with megalomania because I had the audacity to sign my article—this *Neue Freie Presse* is looking forward to a law from a future liberal majority in the lower Austrian Diet that will protect the Vienna Woods!

All in vain! If I am alive for a few more years, I shall make public the story of the battle for the Vienna Woods, with all the details still not known, as well as the five-year battle about the use of the funds designated for the care and education of poor orphans—a battle that the press passed over in dead silence as if in unison. Yes, this press, this perverter of public opinion, carefully avoided any mention of the sanctioning of a law under which almost four million Kronen are allocated yearly for the loftiest of purposes: the rescue of destitute children.

Today as in the past! Times have changed, but villainy has remained the same. Kürnberger, the most significant writer of his day, was forced to publish his essays in the *Korrespondent*—which Count Lamezan called an obscure little local paper—because he found no acceptance among the large newspapers since he would not lend himself to dancing to their tune. Furthermore, he did not want to throw his pearls before swine.

You must edit a periodical of your own in order to give expression to your thoughts; and when I retire from public life—and that will happen within a year's time—I shall have to do the same in order to make public what I have experienced.

Again wishing you tenacity in your battle and a successful outcome, I remain,

Sincerely yours,

Schöffel

Mödling
June 10, 1901

That was in issue no. 81 of *Die Fackel*. In issue no. 78 I had mentioned the *Neue Freie Presse*'s defense of the Vienna Woods and had sent that issue to Joseph Schöffel. My article concluded with the following words:

> Should one not at least be allowed to demand that those whose hands have been accustomed to taking money from lumber swindlers not suddenly talk about the beauty of nature? We do not want to prove apostate to the dogma that God created the forests for the lumber corporations. The forests groan under the ax laid to them so that the blessing of the newspaper page may be brought to a culture-hungry mankind. But it is adding insult to injury if upon the freshly obtained wood-pulp nature is defended instead of corruption.

And in the preface to Schöffel's letter that was to introduce his splendid contributions to *Die Fackel*, I wrote:

> In issue no. 78, when, to gratify the public's need for amusement, I recommended the article in the *Neue Freie Presse* in which the newspaper presented itself as the protector of the Vienna Woods and demanded of a "liberal majority of the Diet" the preservation of natural treasures—nowadays no longer threatened by lumber profiteers but only by heavy downpours—I was hardly aware of how aptly I had struck the nail on the rottenest head in this realm. I confess that it was less the knowledge of the history of the events that took place at the time of the actual battle for the Vienna Woods than it was an instinctive sense of the underhanded dealings, successfully conducted over decades by the leading destroyer of our culture, that induced me to strike at the dirty hands of the *Neue Freie Presse*, which dared to

spread those hands protectively over Vienna's natural
treasures.

At that time I had only the vague feeling that the *Neue Freie
Presse* must formerly have fought in the front ranks of those
newspapers "to whom the stands of forests in the environs of
Vienna were dear exclusively from the point of view of the
lumber profiteer."

And when Schöffel published his *Memoirs* in 1905 he wrote
at the conclusion of the chapter "Concerning the Vienna
Woods":

The *Neue Freie Presse*, at one time the loyal companion
and shield bearer of the syndicate controlling the sale of
government-owned property—the syndicate that wanted
to devastate and sell off the Vienna Woods—published
an article in May, 1901—that is, at a time when no one
thought of injuring the Vienna Woods, let alone devastating them or bartering them away—an article describing
in glowing terms that glorious natural park, the Vienna
Woods, whose preservation in its green splendor is a vital
matter for us Viennese, and concluding with the pious
ejaculation: "Perhaps in more tranquil and peaceful times
there will one day be a majority in the Lower Austrian
Diet of such progressive and truly democratic cast as
to determine on a law for the protection and preservation of the Vienna Woods against devastation and any
other kind of injury."
Using this article the writer Karl Kraus lit into the *Neue
Freie Presse* with his Torch (*Die Fackel*) and gave it a
proper piece of his mind. . . .
Indubitably, after my death, when my tongue has become silent and my arm powerless, there will be all sorts
of tall tales concocted and yarns spun by lying tongues

about the one-time battle for the Vienna Woods! That cannot be helped.

My only wish is that if the Vienna Woods should ever again be threatened by a speculation syndicate—and that is not out of the question—a man will turn up at the opportune moment who will successfully defend the Woods.

May these lines serve him as an arsenal; I have written them down solely for this purpose.

I have the kindest tokens of the interest he maintained in *Die Fackel* to the very end; and what I seized upon from the world of criminal infamy engrossed him as powerfully as did my battles with the press. During the time he was occupied with his memoirs he sent me with his Open Letter in issue no. 170 the following words:

> In the miasma in which we live, a miasma impregnated with moral pestilence, your publications in *Die Fackel* are truly refreshing. You remind me vividly of Kürnberger! Go ahead and get at the gangs of political robbers and their leaders. If anyone today is in a position to scourge these filibusterers it is you!

Half a year before his own death, Robert Scheu wrote an obituary in *Die Fackel* in commemoration of Schöffel's work, concluding with the following words:

> History will show him as one who was strong and courageous and who plunged into the vortex where it raged at its most savage; as one whose works are today still verdant; and as one who came back from the vortex unsullied! Happy is the man who may mention his name without blushing!

Woe to the many who dare to mention his name because they are no longer able to blush!

"Woe unto the posterity that fails to appreciate him!"

TRANSLATED BY SHEEMA Z. BUEHNE

Letters Received in Wartime

[1916]

A letter with a mourning border nameless as its pain. Here set as an epitaph, it means that I reciprocate the thanks and that I honor in one unknown victim all the young men who have been torn out of life.

May 16, 1916

Having completed his university studies, our son Josef joined artillery regiment no. 30. He was, as they say, one of the best and the bravest. On February 29 his fate caught up with him. A second lieutenant, the enemy's bullet hit him while he was at his observer's post. The big silver medal for bravery was mailed to his parents, whose only child and only happiness he was. He rests in Ravence next to the bell tower of the wooden church, and his grave is verdant and blooming.

Karl Kraus!

Accept his last greeting. You did not know him and yet you were the closest to him in this world. He belonged to your community and was your most faithful follower and partisan. How he loved you! Your picture adorns his room, your books ornament it. He avoided talking about you with people who did not appear to him to be worthy. I, his mother, knew what you meant to him.

It is like a holy legacy to me. I had to tell you that he was not unworthy of you.

I am looking at the last issue of *Die Fackel* that I hold in my hands—I could perish from pain and sorrow that his eyes will never again behold it, and that this noble young man had to die for this mankind!

May his last greeting, his last thanks, be dedicated to you, Karl Kraus,

by his mother

TRANSLATED BY FREDERICK UNGAR

Ghosts

[1919]

The President of the National Assembly
of German-Austria*
Vienna, May 1, 1919

Dear Sir:

The completion of the twentieth year since *Die Fackel* began publication prompts me to take this welcome opportunity to express to you my sincerest gratitude for the great work you have done toward the purification and moral and intellectual edification of the Austrian public during these two decades. Particularly your brave, courageous, tenacious struggle against the war and against all the degradation and humiliation it caused will never be forgotten. In your publication moral outrage about the barbarity of the war found its most passionate expression, and power of feeling was wedded to power of form, thus shaping ideas into deeds.

* The name of the territory that, after the collapse of the Austrian-Hungarian monarchy (November 12, 1918), became the Republic of Austria (Republik Österreich) in the peace Treaty of St. Germain.

86

Every supporter of the Republic will gratefully appreciate what your words contributed toward the banishment of old ghosts.

If my congratulations reach you belatedly, please attribute it to the excessive pressures of my work.

Expressing my great esteem,

Seitz

I, too, did not manage until today to thank you, Mr. President, even though a Viennese daily recently branded me an idler, completely contradicting your opinion. This incident may be viewed as proof of how greatly you overvalue my achievement and how little I have actually contributed during two decades to the purification and moral and intellectual edification of the public; and with compelling logic it will become clear how my belief in ghosts is still justified today and how well founded my conviction is that a thousand retired murderers [generals and government officials] do not constitute a revolutionary success if ten journalists can direct our fate.

It is painful for me to have to state to the President of the Republic that people in our country have never been more stupid than since the birth of this Republic. Stupidity will undoubtedly put the blame on the Republic because stupidity, longing for the times that made it stupid, can no longer complete even the briefest thought process. It goes like this: the monarchy brought us the war, war brought us ruin, ruin brought us the Republic. No, stupidity perceives only the simultaneity of Republic and ruin: the Republic brought us ruin.

The reverse process is easier—thus, if possible without the intermediary steps: ruin shall bring us the monarchy. The Republic is to blame for everything, for stupidity, too, and on its very first day it already showed itself incapable of paying the debts of the monarchy, of awakening the monarchy's dead, of undoing the monarchy's war.

Lack of imagination made the war possible; a minimum of imagination is necessary to recognize its causes. Secure in this *circulus vitiosus,* the press continues to plunder all the possessions of defenseless mankind. Nothing better can be wished for mankind, nothing with more fervent longing, than that the Republic, recognizing a blood relationship, would put an end to the surviving parasites of the empire as well as to the spongers on the revolution; that the Republic would finally smash the machines of a trade that is lying the people to death on the infamous pretense of freedom of the press. Only then—so I believe, Mr. President—will the ghosts be banished!

TRANSLATED BY HELENE SCHER

Reply to a Well-Known Woman Writer

[1919]

Vienna, October 7, 1919

Dear Professor:

Mr. K., who thanks you for your letter, to his regret is not, for reasons of principle, in a position to support, by supplying answers to questions, your intention of writing about his works. Apart from that, however, he is of the opinion that the items included in the questionnaire kindly sent him—several of these, like the question regarding birth dates, have already been answered in the *Literatur Kalender*—do not have the slightest bearing on the works of an author, especially not in this case. First and foremost he would have to leave unanswered the question about "Military Service, Campaigns" (not to be confused with the heading "Years of Success") as well as the one about "Medals, Titles, Other Honors, Incidentals."

However, he would not like to conceal from you the fact that he has only a very low opinion of a volume of Literary Biographies for which any such questions as these can be asked of authors, and for which the authors themselves can answer questions like those about "Relationship with Well-Known Persons," "Difficulties Encountered in Career," and the like. Of course, he is far from holding you responsible for the contents of the printed questionnaire drawn up by the Archives of Journalistic Work.

With regard to your own intention of writing about his works, he is, to be sure, of the opinion that up to the stage of its actualization, this is a matter that concerns only the critic and not the subject of such a critique. In again expressing his thanks to you for your kind communication, we remain

Sincerely yours,

Verlag Die Fackel

TRANSLATED BY SHEEMA Z. BUEHNE

"Écrasez l'infâme!"

[1920]

Confronted with the boundless insolence toward our Republic displayed in broad daylight by the most insidious line of swindlers in this country, the black marketeers of public opinion, in a word, the journalists of Jewish and anti-Semitic caliber, who even demand respect for their vile trade, I find myself provoked once again to quote what Kierkegaard vowed in 1846, at a time when the scum of mankind had not yet brought about a World War and survived it:

> "God in Heaven knows that bloodthirstiness is foreign to my soul, and I believe I have to a terrifying degree a sense of responsibility toward God. But nevertheless I would take upon myself, in the name of God, the responsibility of giving the command to open fire if I had assured myself beforehand with the most scrupulous, most meticulous conscientiousness that the guns would be pointed at no human being, indeed, no living creature other than—journalists!"

The applause with which this quote was received evoked from the speaker the retort "Écrasez l'infâme!," a retort that

91

was as little understood as followed. Here in Vienna the proclamation of the "Viennese Press Organization" will undoubtedly make a greater impression than Kierkegaard:

> "At the meeting on the 18th of the Industrial Conference the engineer Mr. Taussig, a spokesman for the subcommittee, objected to what he believed to be the disproportionately large quantity of newsprint produced in German-Austria.* 'It is improper,' he said, 'to allot such enormous sums from our nation's wealth to the *most unproductive activity*, for a purpose *adding up to almost nil.*'
>
> "We for our part consider it improper that a man with such scant knowledge of the world and such backward ideas may be allowed to be the spokesman for German-Austria's industry. *The experiences of this war have sufficiently demonstrated how dearly states and nations will pay if they do not know how to assess correctly the power of the press in contemporary life.* We deem it quite unnecessary to defend the political, cultural, and economic significance of modern newspapers against the ignorance and presumption of a Mr. Taussig. Nevertheless we express our regret that at a meeting as serious as the Industrial Conference no one contradicted such thoughtless and tactless statements."

Never before have professional liars uttered such true words. To be sure, the experiences of this war have sufficiently demonstrated how dearly states and nations will pay if they do not know how to assess correctly the power of the press in all our life today for, if the murder victim had taken precautions, the murderer would have had no power over him. When Kierkegaard cried out his "Woe, woe betide the press!" and himself became guilty of such thoughtless and tactless statements, he also said: "If Christ were to appear in the world today, he would, so help me God, take aim not at the high priests, but at the journalists!" But, in that case, the "Viennese Press Organiza-

* See footnote page 86.

tion" would surely get the better of him, and one of their organs would boast: "In printing this attack against the press, our paper has immediately given the attacker the response he deserves." We have no choice, therefore, at least after the experiences of this war, but to assess correctly the power of the press, to employ to better effect the means recommended by Voltaire against the much less harmful church, and to use force for the sole ethical purpose that states and nations in the future may be spared such force. Écrasez l'infâme!

TRANSLATED BY HELENE SCHER

To the Publishers
of the Brockhaus Encyclopedia

[1921]

Vienna, December 20, 1921

F. A. Brockhaus
Querstr. 16
Leipzig

Mr. Karl Kraus thanks you for your kind invitation to submit a
sketch of his life and activities. However, although he is accustomed to speaking to his own public about everything concerning his activities, he nevertheless has some misgivings about
telling anyone other than passport authorities even so much as
when he was born. But even apart from this obstacle, which is
rather one of principle, now that *Die Fackel* has been appearing for twenty-two years, now that more than a dozen books of
his have gone through several editions, now that several books
about him have been published and two hundred lectures given
by him, he would unfortunately not be in a position to impart
to a lexicon eager for knowledge information as to how he
achieved all this.

Not that, in reverse, he was avidly desirous of obtaining this information at long last from you. But there is nothing that he wishes less today than to furnish autobiographical material and perhaps have it reach the desk of a specialist who by the very belatedness of such a curiosity has already amply demonstrated what, in fact, his position is with respect to the object of his recent interest.

About ten years ago a reader of *Die Fackel*, who had been acquainted with it for a much longer period of time, addressed the publishers of this encyclopedia, without the knowledge of the editor, inquiring how it was at all possible that in the survey of the intellectual life of Vienna the existence of *Die Fackel* was kept from a public that was not denied particulars about the lives of the most insignificant German and Austrian men of letters. The reader passed on to him [Karl Kraus] the rather arrogant reply that the editorial offices would not find it difficult to give an answer to this inquiry; and now he would also like to have the point in time at which your specialist deems a writer worthy of reciting his biography to him.

It is, of course, not at all incomprehensible that a person who wants to keep abreast, so to speak, of the facts of Austrian intellectual life and who considers as complete the list of publications put out by the *Neue Freie Presse* for circulation abroad will occasionally find it disturbing to be suddenly overwhelmed by an unknown fact. However, since the person who is actually concerned has, for his part, long since lost interest, if he ever had any, in being made known to the readers of an encyclopedia, he must regret his inability to accommodate you in this way.

Since your editorial office will perhaps not let itself be deterred, by his indifference on this point, from publishing what it considers worth knowing, he would, at the most, be in a position to protect it against misinformation by referring it to a source from which correct data can be obtained, i.e., the book *Karl Kraus und sein Werk* by Leopold Liegler. For this assistance in matters of pure fact you would most appropriately reciprocate by fulfilling the request that is on his mind, a request to you as well as to all institutions that concern themselves professionally with literary criticism, and that is—in his case—to abstain from it.

Sincerely yours,

Verlag Die Fackel

TRANSLATED BY SHEEMA Z. BUEHNE

The Impact and the Consequences
of the Russian Revolution
on World Culture

An Exchange of Letters

[1924]

Berlin, September 24, 1924

Dear Mr. Kraus:

By order of the editorial office of the Moscow illustrated weekly *Krassnaja Niva*, the most widely circulated literary periodical, edited by Lunacharsky, commissar for the people's enlightenment, and Stekloff, chief editor of *Izvestia*, we turn to you in the following matter.

Krassnaja Niva, on the occasion of the anniversary of the October Revolution, has undertaken an inquiry among the most prominent personalities in the fields of art and literature in order so to determine what the Russian October Revolution of 1917 has achieved for world culture.

The question is: What kind of impact and consequences, in your opinion, has the Russian Revolution had on world culture?

We take the liberty of asking you politely to participate in this inquiry and to send to our office no later than October 10 your esteemed reply—ten to twenty printed lines—if possible with your picture and autograph, which will be published at the same time as the text.

Thank you in advance most cordially. We hope to receive your esteemed reply very soon.

Sincerely yours,

J. Gakin
Representative
of *Izvestia*
and *Krassnaja Niva*

Vienna, October 4, 1924

Dear Mr. Gakin:

The impact and consequences of the Russian Revolution on world culture, in my opinion, consist in the fact that the most prominent representatives in the fields of art and literature are invited by representatives of the Russian Revolution to describe in ten to twenty printed lines, if possible with their picture and autograph, which will be published simultaneously—that is, entirely in the spirit of prerevolutionary journalism—the impact and consequences, in their opinion, of the Russian Revolution on world culture, which can indeed sometimes be done in the prescribed ten to twenty lines.

Sincerely yours,

Karl Kraus

TRANSLATED BY FREDERICK UNGAR

Concerning the Treatment
of the Hebrew Language
in Soviet Russia

[1930]

Berlin, July 15, 1930

Dear Mr. Kraus:

I am taking the liberty of asking you to give the enclosed statement your kind consideration.

I should be grateful if, after examining it, you could decide in favor of lending cogency to an important and worthy cause by adding your signature to the enclosed appeal, which will be submitted to the Soviet government and publicized throughout the world.

Most respectfully and sincerely yours,

Arnold Zweig

P.S. The appeal has already been signed by the following gentlemen: Jakob Wassermann, Arthur Hollitscher, Martin Buber, Ch.N. Bialik, S. Tschernichowski, Jakob Klatzkin, Arnold Zweig.

Please be good enough as to address your reply to Mr. ——.

99

Vienna, July 31, 1930

Dear Sirs:

Mr. Karl Kraus thanks you very much for the kind intention of the request transmitted by Mr. Arnold Zweig but regrets that he is unable to comply with it for the following reasons:

In the first place, in accordance with a statement previously published in *Die Fackel* he must decline to give his position on political-cultural matters that lie outside his own field as writer. Only to appeals or protests that directly serve to render aid to certain threatened people could he affix his signature without regard to the literary persons who co-signed this appeal. In this given instance he would also have to decline for the very reason that, with all due confidence in the information supplied him, he is essentially not acquainted with the subject matter involved; and his advocacy would be tantamount to the presumption of a knowledge and of a relationship that he completely lacks.

In this specific case, it should be said that, as a German writer, he is far less concerned with the suppression of the Hebrew language in the Soviet Union than with that of the German language in Germany. Regardless of what evil and injustice the Department of Jewish Affairs and the Russian government may inflict on the Hebrew language, that, in his opinion, could not remotely approach the persecutions and injuries to which the German language is exposed in editorial offices—a situation that indeed frequently also constitutes a Jewish cultural matter.

Consequently—with all sympathy for your efforts—since his concern is directed rather to the German language, he would not be in a position, even if no fundamental impediment stood in the way of fulfilling your wish, to sign an appeal containing a sentence in which support for the Hebrew language is given at the expense of the German: "Deportations and incarcerations of numerous persons found guilty of teaching and studying the Hebrew language and literature *has* [sic] been established on good authority."

In conclusion we ask you, furthermore, to bear in mind that, apart from all else, Mr. Karl Kraus would not be desirous of linking himself with a group of persons who, with the expression "We, European intellectuals," confer upon themselves an honorary title, which, as long as it is not carried in the register of an association, could be bestowed only by history, and which would first have to be demonstrably justified in each instance.

Again with thanks for your kind intention of enrolling Mr. Karl Kraus in these ranks,

Sincerely,

Verlag Die Fackel

TRANSLATED BY SHEEMA Z. BUEHNE

LIBEL SUITS

Hans Müller's Libel Suit
against Karl Kraus
[1920]

In May, 1917, in Geneva, I read in the *Berliner Tageblatt* a tele-
gram from Vienna reporting that Hans Müller, the author of
Könige (Kings), had instituted a libel suit against the writer
Karl Kraus. Though remote from the happenings of war, I was
nevertheless to feel its influence twice in those summer days
through the death of a friend killed in action and through the
suit of Müller, who had advocated accepting hardships cheerfully. One can more or less imagine my frame of mind when,
soon afterward, I worked on *The Last Days of Mankind.*

When, with my manuscript in my bag, I nevertheless returned to my fatherland, which was then still bristling with all
the perils inherent in the troth of the Nibelungs, I was summoned to court, where the poet [Müller] had already applied
to have the police hunt me down on the grave suspicion that I
was trying to evade being served with the summons. Furthermore, he had followed up his first charge, concerning the article
"Hans Müller in Schönbrunn," with a second, because in the
interim I had had a satirical relapse and written my "Sunday's

Child." I did not deny having written and published both articles, but reserved my defense for the trial.

The judge presiding over the pretrial investigation had known me for years and was one of the kindliest of men, deserving a better fate than growing gray amidst documents relating to proceedings against the press. When I told him that I had evaded the serving of a summons only because I had been staying in the Tödi Valley, I saw the old mountaineer's eyes light up at the mention of the name with such a look of poignant yearning as no feuilleton of Müller's could ever convey. Then I left, so as not to evade being served with the following complaint:

[In this complaint Hans Müller sought the conviction of the accused and also an injunction against further circulation of the article.]

That Hans Müller was not at the front despite the fact that he wrote a description of life at the front, he himself admits, and he supports my assertions through the voluntary deposition of that description, whose literary value I certainly did not mean to deprecate when I stated that it indisputably conveyed the impression of first-hand experience. It really did convey that impression to all readers, especially at a time (fall, 1914) when one could still expect an author glowing with patriotic fervor to feel the urge to experience just that which he was glorifying in such vibrant terms; and now that the plaintiff, through the deposition of the feuilleton "Cassian at War," has relieved me of a considerable burden of my evidence, my only remaining task is to prove that his description made the same impression—altogether estimable from the patriotic standpoint, of course—also upon readers other than myself, and especially upon military readers.

At that time one could no more doubt that Hans Müller was in the field than one could doubt the truth of the story he told in one of his feuilletons, according to which he had embraced and kissed a German soldier and then wept in the *Gedächtnis-kirche* (Memorial Church) in Berlin. If Hans Müller had not wished to convey such an impression—that of personal involvement in the events of war—he would have been better advised not to let himself be totally carried away by the storminess of his feuilletonistic description, but to add a note making it clear from the outset that he was only availing himself of the poet's license to invent experiences. It was, I think, not too ridiculous to assume that a young man writing a description of life at the front was actually in that situation himself.

Nothing was farther from my intention than to offend Herr Müller's honor through this assumption; nor is anything even now farther from my intention than to reproach Herr Müller with actually *not* being at the front. I would have all the less reason for doing so because it is a proven fact that I was not at the front myself, though to be sure I never gave my readers, through a radiant description of life there, the impression that I was. On the other hand, I certainly can document as my own personal experience the grim contrast between the reality of life at the front and the life of those who derive, from the happenings of war, substance for a feuilleton or a good idea for a drama, after writing amusing and risqué stories up until the outbreak of war. I do not know whether this age in which we live and die is such that I should on that account have to defend myself before a public tribunal.

The sole purpose of that sentence which the plaintiff finds incriminating was to assert that, apart from his adventure in front of the panther's cage at Schönbrunn, Herr Müller had actually never since the outbreak of war been in imminent danger of his life. If Herr Müller today says that it would have been "ludicrous" of him to wish to create the impression of having written a description of life at the front while not actually being at the front, my only response is that in future the best way for a writer living on the home front to avoid the crude misinterpretation to which he has been subjected, is to describe the coal shortage instead of the atmosphere around the campfire. Then such confusions as are inevitable in wartime will not recur when, for example, a playwright who wears civilian clothes in Vienna dons a field-gray uniform before bowing to the audience on the evening of his Munich premiere, hence creating the unavoidable impression that he has rushed directly from the trenches to the stage. If today any war-intoxicated young man is guilty of such irresponsibility in the choice of material for both his dramas and his clothes, then he certainly has no right to complain if the rumor spreads that he is in active service at the front or—should people hear that this is not the case—if at least the impression arises that he lays store by the dissemination of such an impression.

The admitted fact that the plaintiff published a feuilleton describing life at the front without having been there facilitates the assumption that his later editorial in the *Neue Freie Presse*, depicting his reception by the German Emperor at the Hofburg in Vienna, might likewise be based on poetic imagination. To be sure, his description in the editorial was so vivid that one could take his audience with the German Emperor to be an actual event, but after one's experience with Herr Müller in the matter of his depiction of life at the front, it seemed advisable to exercise some of that caution he himself had failed to exercise earlier. We had learned that Herr Müller was living in Vienna during the war, and it was a consolation to know that he had been spared for his writing, even though this writing was dedicated exclusively to the glorification of a sphere of activity whose destructive consequences he has not personally experienced.

All the more reasonable then was the assumption that everything Müller wrote during that entire period—with the
possible exception of the episode involving the panther in
Schönbrunn—derived not so much from experience as from
imagination. This *possibility*, and nothing more, explains my
remark concerning his experience at the Hofburg. *Not for one
moment did I actually believe that he had invented this audience.* I was implying that confused readers might be faced with
the necessity of determining what was truth and what was fic-
tion, but *not* that I myself harbored doubts as to the poet's
veracity on this point.

For any reader, and particularly any reader of *Die Fackel*, it
is unambiguously clear from the text and tone of the incriminating passage that my purpose was definitely not literally to
assert that Hans Müller had not been received by the German
Emperor at the Hofburg and that his own statement was therefore an untruth. The imputation that Müller had told a lie
would scarcely have merited an expenditure of satirical effort.
On the contrary, it was my aim to express my dismay that
Müller had told the *truth* when he said that he had been received by the Emperor at the Hofburg. This fact is so palpably
and demonstrably true that I myself could have been cited as
a witness to it, since in the preceding issue of *Die Fackel* I had
even presented an unbelieving world with a special supplement
containing a photographic reproduction of his editorial on the
subject.

Far from wishing to accuse Müller of an untruth, I myself
furnished the proof of his truthfulness which he could now
produce against me, and I had ample though distressing reason
for doing so. It could never be the purpose of this reproduction, which was offered without commentary, which all the
readers of "Hans Müller in Schönbrunn" vividly recalled, and
which was received as a revelation of the *truth* everywhere in
Germany—it could never have been the purpose of this repro-

duction of a title page of the *Neue Freie Presse* to assert that what Müller here maintained was untrue.

On the contrary, I obviously intended to nip in the bud any possible doubts even in future readers and to proclaim to posterity, who otherwise would hardly believe that the German Emperor had received Hans Müller at the Hofburg in Vienna and had spoken highly political words to him: "Yes, indeed, it *did* happen, and if you don't believe it, here's the photo to prove it!"

I countered this danger of later readers distrusting my veracity by including the editorial of the poet of *Könige* as a photographic supplement to *Die Fackel*. That was in the April issue. Consequently, it would have been impossible for me to attempt to maintain in the following issue that Müller had told a *lie*. If in April it was my obvious intention by means of an expensive photographic supplement to lend added circulation and the greatest possible authenticity to Müller's assertion, then in May I cannot—without either transition or explanation—have had the opposite intention. Rather, the stylization of the passage is explained by the intention of discussing something "incredible" whose straightforward presentation would be neither appropriate to the nature of satire nor—in this case—in agreement with the actual facts; this should be clear to anybody capable of reading a satire.

What I wanted to say was: "Müller maintains that the German Emperor received him at the Hofburg in Vienna. *I cannot believe it!* I *cannot* believe it!" When, faced with irrefutable fact, one declares that it is "incredible," one does not mean on that account that it is *not true*. I have not the slightest doubt about the truthfulness of this writer, who, as he has proved, certainly is not lacking in inventiveness but is no liar, and I would not hesitate for one moment to affirm publicly and before any tribunal that Hans Müller did not lie and that I never asserted or tried to assert that he had lied when he related in an editorial of the *Neue Freie Presse* that the German Emperor had received him at the Hofburg.

To be sure, it might appear strange that the Emperor had bestowed such a distinction upon an author not writing at the front, since it is a known fact that, without exception, the writers most favored by Kaiser Wilhelm II hold military rank—like Majors Lauff and Höcker, and Captain Walter Bloem—and that Ganghofer was after all a front-line correspondent and, as everyone knows, was even exposed to danger. For many a reader the only explanation remaining may well be that the Kaiser had just read Hans Müller's feuilleton "Cassian at War" and had believed that the poet had already earned his spurs. Yet, surprised though I was at the fact of this audience, I did not doubt for one moment that it had taken place.

One might almost have expected Müller himself, in defense of higher interests, to offer the sacrifice of a confession that he had lied and that the audience had not taken place. Only he, and no one else, would have the right, perhaps the patriotic duty, to deny the reliability of his earlier statement. If he does not do so and lays store by people believing it and consequently by the acknowledgment of the fact of that exciting audience, then I am the last person in the world who would stand in his way. I have no hesitation then in expressing my sincere regrets at a misunderstanding which, had it really occurred, can be attributed only to the deficiencies of my pen, which, even while attempting valiantly to do justice to both truth and patriotism, was inevitably lacking in the former. That Hans Müller was with Wilhelm II at the Hofburg is as true as the fact that he was not at the front, but instead with the panther in Schönbrunn. Furthermore, this is one of the few truths afforded us German readers since August, 1914.

Karl Kraus

The settlement proceedings scheduled as normal by the court for April 10th had a peculiar outcome, the court record of which the plaintiff declared himself willing to waive as magnanimously as he did his complaint.

Finally the following happened:

The Criminal Court, Vienna, found that proceedings had fallen under the statute of limitations and charged the cost to the plaintiff.

I did not try to evade this summons. It had not lain within the power of the defendant to stay the statute of limitations.

A not unimportant role in the trial had been reserved for the following theater review, which appeared in the *Munich Post* for March 3, 1917, and which is of historical interest not only on account of the dramatist who is reviewed but on account of the reviewer who had signed only with his initials:

> Burgtheater. *Könige* by Hans Müller. Alas, there was no one to occupy the vacant position of German *poeta laureatus*. Formerly it had been occupied by the author of *Charley's Aunt*, but that is past, if for no reason other than that he was an Englishman. (Despite this, Vienna is playing *Charley's Aunt* at present in order to recover from Hans Müller!) Then came Major von Lauff. Silence shrouds his name. Finally, after an anxious pause, we have yet another: Hans Müller, the Viennese playwright from Brünn, responsible for several previous misdeeds on the stage of the Burgtheater, but now *poeta laureatus* elect by virtue of his *Könige*, a play in blank verse. Cotta, who once deigned to publish Goethe, is now sheltering Hans Müller's *Könige* under his roof. Cotta sends the book out into the world with a critical notice, in which we can read, for instance, what the Leipzig mouthpiece of the Crown Prince wrote: 'By far the most mature dramatic product of the war to date.' A literary periodical is even cited with the ominous words: 'This drama will be acted wherever there is a German theater.' (This was meant ironically, however, for it was quoted through misunderstanding from a review ridiculing the play.)

Dressed in field-gray but based in Vienna, Hans Müller has indulged himself lucratively in the mood of the front line. Behind the lines, he read Uhland's hundred-year-old *Ludwig the Bavarian*, a play which was once rejected by the Munich Court Theater and in which Uhland made an early avowal of pan-Germanic convictions. Hans Müller, whose play had better luck with the Burgtheater than Uhland's, adapted this play, making of it a war drama celebrating solidarity between kinsmen. Consequently, matters proceed in a most kingly fashion:

> Whoe'er drew breath in hall of German kings,
> Whoe'er but touched the Empire's diadem,
> Is more than prince of any other land.

Of the German people it is said:

> As each trusts each and sees the azure heavens
> Reflected in each other's bright blue eyes,
> Each gives himself wholly to common cause.

A widow whose husband was killed in war writes that she has fourteen children by him:

> Fourteen! !
> The stork, that German bird . . .

That is how uproarious Hans Müller's German humor is. And his German ethics pronounce it to be a man's most sacred duty to keep his word and covenant, and to permit no hardship or coercion to prevent him from fulfilling that duty.

It is distressing that expressive actors like young Herr Jansen should bestow feelings on such marionettes as these, as if they were dealing with a poetic creation and not merely with the wartime surrogate poetal. . . .

The audience applauded, and Hans Müller flitted across the stage in field-gray uniform.

K. E.*

* See footnote page 115.

Since Goethe, there has probably been no German poet who has associated as frequently as Hans Müller with those personages who, like poets, are wont to dwell on the lofty heights overlooking humanity. And since everyone knows that a man like Müller, having drawn breath in the hall of German kings and touched the Empire's diadem, is more than a prince of any other land, one can easily imagine how small I felt when he, every inch a King, confronted me in that chamber of the court.

Overwhelmed by the feeling of my own nonentity in having written only *The Last Days of Mankind* and not a more stageable drama, I sat there and thought how even the opportunity of reaching out my hand in the direction of an imperial diadem would soon have passed. What greatly blessed mortal, who in his life as a poet surely had no reason to complain, demanded satisfaction of me and overwhelmed me with the assurance, which I found entirely credible, that "he was sitting opposite Karl Kraus for the first, and possibly also the last time"? That is what he should have told his potentates. What did he want from me? Wilhelm stayed until the end of the performance and honored him with even more attention later. Ludwig summoned the poet to his box. There was no denying that either, so what more did he want? He was not only the poet of *Könige*, but the poet of kings; he had not only written *Könige*, but had had the privilege of seeing it produced before a company of kings. When the time came that the kings were on the way out—small wonder, considering such dramatic use and such dramatic taste—he attracted the attention of yet another personage,* who was destined soon to topple a German throne, so that one might say that a subsequent head of state pulled Müller's *Kings* to pieces.

---

* Kurt Eisner (1867–1919) triggered the revolution in Munich in 1918 and became Minister President of the Bavarian Republic.

Whether it is more honorable to be praised by a Wittelsbach
or to be censured by the President of the Bavarian Republic, is
unclear; but it is at any rate a fascinating literary-historical fact
that the author of that spontaneous declaration which I have
quoted above was none other than Kurt Eisner. Had it come
to a trial, I could have referred to his testimony at a time when
Müller's crowned witnesses had already been eclipsed.

Can a man already occupying his place in the sun not be
comforted by the thought that it is sheer envy when I call him
a Sunday child? What did he want from me?—from me, who
can offend no man's honor, whose opinion and reputation,
whose life and activities unfold outside of that world in which
a man has stature and in which groups are formed in order to
confirm his stature. Simply to ignore the occurrence, to turn
away, and to continue on one's straight and narrow path is the
only dignified response to conduct whose paltry significance
scarcely suffices ingloriously to fill thirty recitation halls a
year, so that no Viennese man of letters would find a seat, while
the recognized writers of Vienna, if they joined forces in order
to achieve one single failure, would feel assured that the press's
resounding applause would compensate them.

Until now such writers have been genteel enough to restrain
their raging curiosity about my public readings, and so far not
one of the crowd responsible for the daily theatrical and literary columns has been seen in my audience. If, in fact, they ever
do allow themselves to be enticed into reading *Die Fackel*, they
surely have seen to it that they do so behind closed doors. Again
and again in their private statements one hears them complain
that they are defenseless against me because they have only
the *Neue Freie Presse* at their disposal. However, when the
craftier among them summon up courage for a rejoinder, one
witnesses only the impotent fury of their shameful anonymity—
for they refuse even to call their adversary by name, an offense

which, as occasion offers, I shall repay by giving the cowardly rascals the name that they deserve: to wit, their own.

Yet it is proper that my name is not part of their vocabulary though it may have long since become one of the moral and spiritual possessions of a better humanity uncontaminated by the press, and it is fitting, too, that "one" should take no notice of my existence since I give myself none and since the world may perish before one of these practitioners of the black art receives a free ticket or a review copy from me. For there is no path leading from me into the realm of business and fraud, and on that account the way back from them to me is still less negotiable. How is it possible, then, that from time to time someone whose honor has been offended undertakes to confirm my existence?

I am constantly astonished that people who live on as characters in *The Last Days of Mankind* are still actually alive, and that instead a hole is not burned in the universe where they once had existed in body. Only one party, they or I, can exist at any one given moment. And for that reason, Müller's waiver of a public confrontation in court—which could only have nourished the misconception that I had meant him—was an appropriate though late acknowledgment of the true state of affairs.

I was already disappointed at the pre-trial examination. I had imagined him more kingly in appearance, his purple cloak less distinguishable as Brünn* merchandise. His lawyer often had to caution him to control himself when he threatened to falter in his manly pride (which he had certainly maintained in the presence of kings) in favor of adopting that stance of universal brotherly love which the litterateurs of the War Archives have learned in addition to their other accomplishments (though

* Town in Moravia, known for its textile industry.

only since the conclusion of peace). He spoke from the heart, appealed to my better instincts, and assured me that after my satire even his closest acquaintances had doubted whether Wilhelm had really received him at the Hofburg, thinking that perhaps he had only been received on the train, if at all. With that calm that never fails me at historic moments, I declared myself prepared to make whatever assurances he desired, but even then the storm of emotion would not abate, so that the judge and lawyers lamented this extravagant waste of sentiment on the facts of the case which had already been fully clarified. No, this was no adversary, no polemical partner. For polemics the target must be as qualified as the polemicist.

It was not until I actually saw Müller that I realized how little I had against him. No, he is surely one of the more harmless representatives of our cultural life. And I must say that in court it took all the unbending sternness of an accused man to repulse such familiarity as welled up at moments of intense comradeship, when Müller began to talk man to man, desiring only "not to have Karl Kraus brought in front of a jury." An understandable desire, whose fulfillment had been delayed somewhat through the filing of a libel action.

Yet the simple fact of the matter is that he was born on the sunny side of life, and he seemed determined to pull me over into the sun too. He seemed to have forgotten that he had wanted the police to pursue me to the shades of hell in order to bring me to justice. When the plaintiff insisted on settling the case in this emotional manner—though I would not have been averse to seeing his withdrawal of the complaint officially recorded (and especially to seeing my admission regarding his audience recorded)—all persons present were unanimous that the meeting with Wilhelm at the Hofburg must have been more dignified, to be sure, but that the encounter with the panther at Schönbrunn could hardly have been so exciting.

Astonished at the vast range of personalities accommodated
by German literature, the judge gazed wide-eyed after this liti-
gant who appeared to have obtained complete satisfaction from
receiving permission to withdraw. If, before filing his indictment, Müller had spoken to me instead of to his lawyer, I would
have advised him against it. He would on that occasion have
learned that I hold nothing against him, that I don't reproach
him for his talent and don't blame him for my wit. Apprised in
advance of the essential difference between satire and libel,
Hans Müller would certainly have refrained from taking me to
court and nourishing for a year the hopes of interested parties
in the entire German press that my hour of reckoning had now
come.

Yet what would a conviction against me prove anyway?—
a man who has nothing to lose in the world under whose standards of honor war litterateurs thrive, and who would lose nothing in the world that respects him, since it does respect him
for the very reason of his alleged offense. If I appear in court,
it is because I welcome any forum from which I can direct my
campaign against irresponsible journalism, even a forum which
transforms my ideas into the most crudely materialistic form.

However unpredictable the outcome of the suit, my adversary would surely not relish its proceedings. Since the course
of the suit would hurt my adversary, but its outcome in no case
hurt me, the only satisfaction remaining to him would be to
have financial or physical harm inflicted on me. What if it were
a fine? I can recoup the loss more easily than another man
could through gambling—simply by holding one more public
reading for the benefit of a charity, namely, for the poor of the
city of Vienna. What if I were sent to prison? Do you think it
is any healthier at the Sirk Corner*—where one encounters

---

* Meeting place and promenade across the street from the
Vienna Opera House.

Herr Müller at the very moment one is trying to avoid being served with a summons, or that I would not rather go to prison than see Müller's *Sterne* (Stars)? Or do you think that I would come out reformed? Even if I had experienced the fall of kings while in prison, I could not have refrained, once free, from commenting on the diabolical irony of the fact that the Republic is inaugurating its State Theater with a play by Hans Müller, and that Galileo's tragedy of conscience is calculated to disappoint the war profiteers in their royal box in no way other than that it withholds the climactic line that they have been expecting all evening.

Though field-gray may have been not only the color of infinite suffering but the distinguishing mark of a playwright blessed with royalties; though enraptured kings in the last hours during which they were permitted to dwell on the heights of an ungrateful humanity may have reveled in the feeling that Germany once more had a poet because Austria still had one more feuilletonist—no adversity would have kept me from furnishing that mockery which revises the verdicts of justice as well as the verdicts of the world. As long as the sun of favor shines upon such as Müller, my word, small though it may be, will continue to circle around this problem. Satire does not stand still, and those who wish that it would, will hear instead of the recantation they demanded—unexpected and yet familiar, the cry: "And yet it does move!"

TRANSLATED BY EDWARD MORNIN

[Alice Schalek visited the front lines during World War I as a war correspondent. Her activities there were caustically depicted by Kraus in *The Last Days of Mankind*, as well as in the pages of *Die Fackel.—Editor's note*]

Alice Schalek's Libel Suit against Karl Kraus

[1920]

In the libel suit filed in Vienna in the District Criminal Court, the writer Alice Schalek applied for the prosecution and conviction of the defendant Karl Kraus and for a ban on further distribution of the article that appeared in the May 5, 1916 issue of *Die Fackel*, in which the plaintiff was designated as, among other things, "one of the worst war atrocities that have been committed in this war against the dignity of man"; and further, as "presenting the spectacle of a degeneracy showing the situation of our particular culture as one far worse than that of the rest of Europe."

Against this Karl Kraus filed the following Objection.

Even if it were not for the numerous inquiries that for years have been coming in with regard to the matter of the two trials that originated out of war issues, the history of *Die Fackel* and along with it the picture of journalistic activity in the World War would be incomplete if the files and the material principally connected therewith were not recorded here, as is legally permissible only after the completion of the cases.

Section 1 makes it possible for the Appellate Court to ignore the indictment when "the deed with which the accused is charged does not constitute a culpable action subject to the jurisdiction of the courts." In my judgment this condition is in ample degree fulfilled by the intention and point of view of the incriminating article. No reader of these observations, or of the others that I devoted to the greatly deplored evil of war reportage in general and to the behavior of the plaintiff in particular, could gain the impression that I was concerned with attacking individual persons, and not, quite to the contrary, with discussing one of the many cultural abuses that, as painful concomitant phenomena of a tragic event, have veritably forced themselves upon the grievously tried present time.

In fact, it is also clearly evident from the emphatic and heartfelt statements that have come from all parts of Austria and Germany, and particularly from the front lines, in response to my presentation of this abuse, that the public, and especially those primarily concerned, had valued in those attacks not the personal, but the factual, that is to say, the cultural-critical element. Officers of all ranks who had had the opportunity of observing from immediate proximity the activity of the plaintiff have made manifest to me their grateful and indeed their enthusiastic understanding of a cleansing action, the purpose of which is to protect the battlefield from the sensation-greedy inroads of home-front journalists.

In order to produce the motive for libel, the indictment must make a marked shift. The plaintiff, whom it was not my intention to insult personally in my presentation, must allege that she had been attacked "in her distinctive characteristic of being a woman." The very conception, strange as it is, that being a woman is only a *distinctive characteristic* of woman rehabilitates the intention of my presentation and justifies my attack. The plaintiff was not attacked in her distinctive characteristic of being a woman but in her distinctive characteristic as a man, that is to say, as a newspaper war correspondent.

As far as the person of the plaintiff comes under consideration at all, only two things can be deduced from my criticism: the vigorous repudiation of the bizarre war correspondent, and the protection of woman from an unbefitting activity that will automatically compromise her.

The plaintiff mentions that only a "small circle" of people has any relish for my presentations. This comment, in itself by no means insulting, should not, however, permit her to forget that the much greater circle of people who read her own dispatches has formed no different judgment of these very articles, Kraus's or hers, as is apparent from the statement of a Vienna newspaper,* subjoined under A, which I quote not because I find its alliance gratifying but in order that evidence may be brought of how generally widespread is the view for which the plaintiff is reproaching me. She is completely in error if she considers the incriminating sentences as attacks upon her womanly honor—sentences that, on the contrary, I intended fully as much to protect from their employment in a highly unbefitting profession as to remove what is, after all, obviously the most male of activities from female curiosity.

However, the fact that it is impossible for an action recognized as conservative, useful, and patriotic in the noblest sense to contain simultaneously an element of criminality; and further, that it is precisely the exceptional event in which this action has its roots that necessitates an exceptional assessment of the case—it is in the light of the foregoing that the Objection may refer for support to Section 3 of Paragraph 213. As detailed above, there are on hand sufficient "circumstances by virtue of which the culpability of the deed is denied or the

---

* *Neues Wiener Journal*, July 10, 1916.

prosecution on that account ruled out." But this is the case for yet another simple, extrinsic reason, which in turn is also the result of the exceptional nature of the situation in which the alleged insult takes place. This situation is the state of war. It makes it impossible for the defendant to have the evidence, which the indictment formally requested him to produce, submitted in proper form for courtroom presentation.

However, since the plaintiff opposes this point of view, it would certainly also be necessary to interrogate the most immediately involved and authoritative circles as to the impression which the personality of the plaintiff herself—and not just her literary activity—left them with. How this, despite the ready willingness of numerous witnesses from military circles, should be possible within the given period of time is a mystery. It is far easier for a woman war correspondent to get into a trench than for those whose business it is to be there to get to a Viennese courtroom; and without the personal interrogation of such unobjectionable witnesses, carrying the trial through seems to the defendant to be impracticable.

Technical and, in a higher sense, moral/ethical considerations appear to make it impossible to carry this matter through to a conclusion, at least for the duration of the war, even though the plaintiff herself has no misgivings about submitting her statements to judicial proof. Not least of all, this readiness might in itself be part of the proof.

For if the plaintiff feels hurt by the statement that her activity affords a "spectacle of degeneracy," such an impression will certainly not be mitigated by her propensity to make herself the object of a court sensation in the midst of the World War. She ought to be content with the explanation that her opinion that she had suffered insult to her honor was in error—just as her activity as war correspondent is an aberration. Likewise, she cannot lack the insight that the fulfillment of her desire for satisfaction through a lawsuit is at this time impossible, if it were possible under other circumstances, and that, besides the existence of grave technical obstacles, the sentiment of the public is now dedicated to more profound interests, just as these interests themselves oppose such a trial.

The answer to the complaint is based on the conviction that the Appellate Court will duly evaluate the arguments that have been presented and will above all concede to the defendant, as author of the incriminating article, those very motives, far removed from any criminality, on which those people who have a true ethical interest have felt moved to bestow their unequivocal approval. For those extraordinarily "legitimate interests" that would, at least today, cause the settlement of the case to become a national scandal, are indeed none other than those he has acted to safeguard.

Karl Kraus

The answer, like all briefs entered before the Supreme Court, was unsuccessful.

A hearing had taken place but, as was clear from the outset, a continuance was granted to seek further evidence. Months and years passed, day after day pregnant with unholy glory. And many of those who made no secret of their approval of my action were killed in battle. What a horrible investigation among a group of professionals whose experience included the death of him who had to give evidence about them! In the meantime the description of cleaned-out trenches continued; in the Concert Hall of Vienna the daring woman war reporter's photographs of dead bodies were being shown to an enraptured gang of generals; the district attorney confiscated from me the daily press list of those present; and madmen drove school children there for visual instruction in patriotism. In the meantime letters from the front piled up in which those whose business it was to be there thanked me for the echo of their muteness and for the fact that my purpose was to guard them against those who had no business there but who nevertheless were not forbidden admittance, and most of all that I wanted to guard them against the pain of knowing that their suffering and dying might take place before the eyes of a woman. What this war had been and this home front, what this general staff and what this press, if one has not experienced it himself or found out about it from me, he could learn from the letters that reached me from the front lines; and also what *Die Fackel* meant to the men whom those misbegotten powers sent living to hell. A letter in which the gap between a juridical trifle and the problem of civilization was correctly understood reads as follows:

Vienna, November 5, 1916

Dear Sir:

A section of the Vienna press brought the news that the writer Alice Schalek had brought an action of libel against you.

I am sending you two postcards that reached me from a soldier fighting on the Isonzo front. These postcards, written without knowledge of the fact that Alice Schalek was giving lectures illustrated by photographs of the war theater, express in simple words the moral anger that the extended activity of this woman war correspondent has roused in men.

I myself have studied law and practice the profession that represents the sad result of this course of study; nevertheless, from the earliest years of my youth there has remained with me the idea of the sacredness of the law as the objective reality of true morality.

I am all the more terribly affected that you, who, with unprecedented power, gives form in this age to a most profound, most pure morality, are to be summoned before a court of law to stand trial for an infringement of the law.

The contents of the postcards from the front that I sent you today, as well as the contents of other letters that must be reaching you from the front and from the home front—because the soul of mankind cannot be killed even in the presence of murder and money-making—should be a signpost for the judge who is forced by official duty into the hazardous enterprise of sitting in judgment over you, and should remind him that justice, which is pronounced by him in individual cases, is not in opposition to what those people think and feel who, by risking their lives, make the administration of justice possible.

I am quite well aware that letters like the present one go against your frequently expressed wish. Nevertheless, as one who since the beginning of the war has lived on the home front as a nonparticipant, knowing his near and dear ones without exception to be on the battlefield, and seeing how people performing a hard duty are cheated of their lives by those who, failing to perform that same duty, cheat life and even profit and prosper thereby—I have undertaken this letter to transmit a token of sincere gratitude for the fact that you are here and for what you are doing.

Permit me to express my especial respect and esteem.

The day of the trial came. For Austria. I was simply summoned on April 10, 1918, to a settlement hearing; I refused to give any further explanation but referred to the filed brief containing my complete defense, no other than the one I was able to give at the hearing. The trial scheduled at that time was postponed indefinitely on account of the plaintiff's illness. At a time once more appointed for a settlement attempt only the counsel appeared.

Thus it was a decision in which the court realized both a procedural possibility and the deeply felt impossibility of carrying through to trial when it decided to summon me to account in the preliminary proceedings, and now allowed the very statement contained in the brief to be presented at my interrogation.

After I had again dictated to the clerk what had lain in the file, precisely what had not sufficed three years earlier now appeared enough to bring the trial to an end.

VIENNA DISTRICT CRIMINAL COURT

Pr. II 43/16/66

44

DECISION

The Judiciary Panel of the District Court in Vienna in today's closed session, after hearing from the district attorney's office, rendered the following decision:

The criminal proceedings instituted on the petition of Mrs. Alice Schalek against Mr. Karl Kraus because of the misdemeanor of libel are quashed in pursuance of the withdrawal of the indictment in accordance with Par. 227 STPO.

The plaintiff is to bear the costs of the criminal proceedings, pursuant to Par. 390 STPO.

Vienna, January 25, 1919
Signed: Heidt

This decision did more than any verdict could have done to rehabilitate the quality of woman. The figure emerging will go down in the history of the period, a figure that I could retract only if I could undo the events of those years, which cannot be forgiven and forgotten. Now, however, the private person is divorced from the action and has voluntarily erected that barrier that no writer on earth would have been less willing than I to cross. It was better to triumph over oneself than to triumph over me.

Oh, that a war could be ended like a trial, with dignity and without bloodshed! Oh, that, like a lawsuit, an ultimatum could be withdrawn, one that led to a woman's following the path of war from which so many men will not return.

TRANSLATED BY SHEEMA Z. BUEHNE

DRAMA
The Last Days of Mankind

The following scenes are taken from the translation of *The Last Days of Mankind*, abridged version, issued by Ungar in 1974. The translation is by Alexander Gode and Sue Ellen Wright.

Act I

SCENE 1

Vienna. The Ringstrasse promenade at the Sirk Corner. Flags fly from the buildings. Rousing cheers for troops marching by. General excitement. The crowd breaks up into small groups.

FIRST NEWSBOY: Extra-a-a! Extra-a-a-a!

SECOND NEWSBOY: Extra-a-a! Bo-o-oth official reports!

A DEMONSTRATOR (*breaking away from a group that is singing the "Prince Eugen" march. His face heavily flushed, he has shouted himself hoarse*): Down with Serbia! Down with Serbia! Hurrah for the Hapsburgs! Hurrah! Hurrah for S-e-r-bia!

AN INTELLECTUAL (*noticing the mistake, pokes him sharply in the ribs*): Do you know what you are saying?

DEMONSTRATOR (*first bewildered, then pulling himself together*): Down with S-e-r-bia! Down with the Serbians! Hurrah! Down with the Hapsburgs! S-e-r-b-i-a!

(*In a thronging second group including a Streetwalker, a Hoodlum walking right behind her is trying to snatch her purse.*)

131

HOODLUM (*shouting incessantly*): Hurrah! Hurrah!

STREETWALKER: Keep your hands off me, you bastard! Hands off, or I'll—

HOODLUM (*giving up*): Why aren't you cheering? You call yourself a good Austrian? What you are is a whore. Remember that!

STREETWALKER: And you're a purse snatcher!

HOODLUM: What a slut! There's a war on and don't you forget it! You're a whore, that's what you are.

FIRST PASSER-BY: Keep it down, why don't you? Keep it down!

CROWD (*getting interested*): It's a whore. What did she say?

SECOND PASSER-BY: If I heard her right, she made a crack against our hereditary ruling house.

CROWD: Let's get her! Let's give it to her! (*The girl succeeds in making her escape through a house with a rear exit.*) Oh, let her go! We're not that kind of people. Hurrah for the Hapsburgs!

FIRST REPORTER (*to his colleague*): There's a variety of moods here. What's going on?

SECOND REPORTER: We'll see.

(*Two Army Contractors have climbed up on one of the benches that line the Ringstrasse.*)

FIRST ARMY CONTRACTOR: We can see them better from here. How beautifully they march by. Our brave boys!

SECOND ARMY CONTRACTOR: Bismarck is quoted in today's *Presse*. He says that our people are just kissable.

FIRST ARMY CONTRACTOR: Did you hear they've taken even Eisler's oldest boy?

SECOND ARMY CONTRACTOR: That's unheard of. Rich people like that! Couldn't they have done something about it?

FIRST ARMY CONTRACTOR: I hear they're trying to now. He'll probably go up and fix it.

SECOND ARMY CONTRACTOR: And if worse comes to worse—you'll see, now he'll buy that car the boy's had his heart set on.*

FIRST ARMY CONTRACTOR: And that's another way you can get hurt.

AN OFFICER (*to three other officers*): Hello, Novotny. Hello, Pokorny. Hello, Povolny. Well, Povolny, you're the one who knows politics. What have you got to say?

SECOND OFFICER (*carrying a cane*): If you ask me, it's all because of the encirclement.

THIRD OFFICER: You know—well, of course.

FOURTH OFFICER: That's just how I see it. God, what a night I had. Did you see Schönpflug's newest cartoon? It's a classic.

THIRD OFFICER: You know, the paper said the whole thing is incapable.

SECOND OFFICER: Inescapable, you mean.

THIRD OFFICER: Yes, of course—inescapable. I must have read it wrong. How are things with you?

FOURTH OFFICER: Well, you know, I've got a chance for a desk job at the War Ministry.

FIRST OFFICER: Good work. Then you will be coming in with us. Listen, last night while I was taking in the Mela Mars show at the Apollo, I ran into Novak of the Fifty-ninth. He told me he'd heard they've put me in for the silver medal.

NEWSBOY: *Tagblatt!* Great victory near Scha-a-abaa-atz!

FOURTH OFFICER: Congratulations! (*Turns to look at a passing girl.*) Say, did you see that? A tasty morsel that. (*Goes after her.*)

---

* Possession of an automobile was rare in Austria at that time, and a young man who brought one into the army with him could expect to be assigned to a soft job.

OTHERS (*calling after him*): See you then at Hopfner's.

A GIRL: My Poldl's promised me a Serb's liver for our supper. I've sent that letter in to the editor of the *Reichspost*.

A VOICE: Hurrah for the *Reichspost*! Our Christian daily!

ANOTHER GIRL: I sent in a letter too! My Ferdy'll bring me the kidneys of a Russian.

AN INTELLECTUAL (*to his Girl Friend*): Here in this very spot you could delve deeply into the soul of the people, if we only had more time. What time is it? This morning's editorial says, "living is a joy." Brilliant, when he says that all the glory of classical greatness sheds its radiance upon our time.

GIRL FRIEND: It's half past. Mother said I'll catch it if I get home after half past.

INTELLECTUAL: Come on, stay. Look at the people. There's a ferment in the air. Just watch the uplift!

GIRL FRIEND: Where?

INTELLECTUAL: I mean of the soul. How ennobled the people are! As the editorial says, "every man a hero." Who would have believed times could have changed so—and we with them.

(*A horse-drawn cab pulls up in front of a house.*)

PASSENGER: How much do you get?

CABBY: The gentleman knows.

PASSENGER: No, I don't. How much do you get?

CABBY: Well, just what the fare is.

PASSENGER: What is the fare?

CABBY: Well, just what you give to the others.

PASSENGER: Can you change this? (*Hands him a ten-kronen gold piece.*)

CABBY: Change it? I wouldn't take even the whole thing! It could be French money.

A Concierge (*walking over to them*): What? A Frenchman? Well, what do you know? He could be a spy! We'll give it to him! Where did he come from?

Cabby: From the East Terminal.

Concierge: Ah, from Saint Petersburg!

Crowd (*which has collected around the cab*): A spy! A spy! (*The Passenger disappears into the house with a rear exit.*)

Cabby (*shouting after him*): What a shady bastard!

Crowd: Oh, let him go. No reprisals! That's not right. We're not like that!

An American Representative of the Red Cross (*to his companion*): Just look at these people. How enthusiastic they are!

Crowd: Two Englishmen! Speak German! May God punish England! Let 'em have it! We're in Vienna! (*The Americans escape into the house with a rear exit.*) Oh, let 'em go. We're not like that!

A Turk (*to another Turk*): Regardez l'enthousiasme de tout le monde.

Crowd: Two frogs! Speak German! Let 'em have it! We're in Vienna! (*The Turks escape into the house with a rear exit.*) Oh, let 'em go. We're not like that! Listen, that was Turkish. Don't you see they're wearing fezzes. They're our allies. Catch up with them and let's sing the "Prince Eugen" march for them.

(*Two Chinese enter. They keep silent.*)

Crowd: Some Japs are here! Japs still in Vienna! The bastards should be strung up by their pigtails.

First: Leave them alone. Those are Chinks!

Second: You're a Chink yourself!

First: Maybe you are!

Third: All Chinks are Japs!

FOURTH: Are you a Jap maybe?

FIFTH: Now then, now then! What are you doing? Haven't you read the paper? (*Unfolds a newspaper*). Just look, here it says, "Such excesses of patriotism can in no way be tolerated. Furthermore, they are liable to harm tourist traffic." How is tourist traffic supposed to develop if this kind of thing goes on!

SIXTH: Bravo! He's right. If we want to increase the tourist traffic—that's hard, it's not easy to do—

SEVENTH: Shut up! War's war, and if somebody jabbers American or Turkish or something—

EIGHTH: Right! There's a war on, and this is not the time to fool around.

(*A lady with a trace of a moustache appears.*)

CROWD: Ah, look at that! We weren't born yesterday. A spy in disguise! Arrest her! Lock her up, quick.

A LEVEL-HEADED MAN: Just a minute, gentlemen—just consider—she could have gotten a shave.

ONE OF THE CROWD: Who?

LEVEL-HEADED MAN: If she were a spy.

SECOND: He forgot to. And so he's trapped himself.

SHOUTS: Who? —He! —No, she!

THIRD: That's just one of those tricks spies have.

FOURTH: They let their beards grow so that we won't notice that they're spies.

FIFTH: Don't be so dumb. That's a female spy, and she's stuck on a beard so that we won't catch on.

SIXTH: It's a female spy trying to pass herself off as a man.

SEVENTH: No, it's a man passing himself off as a female spy.

CROWD: In any case he's a shady character who should be taken to the precinct. Grab him!

(*The lady is led away by a policeman. One hears the singing of "The Watch on the Rhine."*)

FIRST REPORTER (*notebook in hand*): This was no flare-up of
intoxicated momentary enthusiasm, no noisy outburst of
morbid mass hysteria. With genuine manliness Vienna accepts the fateful decision. Do you know how I would sum up
its mood? Its mood might be summed up in the words:
far from haughtiness and far from weakness. Far from
haughtiness and far from weakness—this phrase, which we
have coined to describe the dominant mood of Vienna, cannot be repeated too often. Far from haughtiness and far
from weakness. Well, what do you think of my stuff?

SECOND REPORTER: What should I say? Brilliant!

FIRST REPORTER: Far from haughtiness and far from weakness.
Thousands upon thousands of people have marched through
the streets today arm in arm; rich and poor, young and old,
high and lowly. Everyone's bearing showed that he was
fully aware of the solemnity of the situation but also proud
to feel throbbing in his own body the pulsebeat of the
great era about to break upon us.

VOICE FROM THE CROWD: Kiss my ass!

FIRST REPORTER: Listen to the "Prince Eugen" march and the
Austrian national anthem being played over and over again,
and with these two, as a matter of course, "The Watch on
the Rhine," in keeping with the Nibelung troth.° Today
Vienna has stopped working earlier than usual. Oh, and
don't let me forget. We must especially describe how the
public was massing in front of the War Ministry. But most
of all, we must not forget to bring out—guess what?

° Loyalty to the death. A reference to the medieval Nibelung
saga, used by Wagner as the basis for the operas in his *Ring*
cycle.

SECOND REPORTER: How could I not know? We must not forget to bring out that hundreds upon hundreds of people massed on the Fichtegasse in front of the building of the *Neue Freie Presse.*°

FIRST REPORTER: A great mind you've got! Yes, that's what the boss likes. But what do you mean "hundreds upon hundreds?" Did you count them? Why don't you say "thousands upon thousands?" What do you care since they are massing anyway? Then they roared thundering cheers—to Austria, Germany, and the *Neue Freie Presse*. The sequence wasn't exactly flattering for us, but still it was very nice of the enthusiastic crowd. All evening they stood pressed tightly and were massing on the Fichtegasse unless they had something to do in front of the War Ministry or on the Ballhausplatz.†

SECOND REPORTER: I can't imagine where people get the time.

FIRST REPORTER: The time is so great that there's time left over for it.

SECOND REPORTER: The big thing now is street scenes. From every street curb where there's a dog demonstrating he‡ wants a street scene. He called me in yesterday and told me I should observe human interest scenes. But that's exactly what I find disagreeable. I hate getting mixed up in a crowd. Yesterday I had to join in singing "The Watch on the Rhine." Let's get away from here. Things might start getting out of control. Just look at them. I know this mood. All of a sudden you're caught up in it, and before you know it, you're singing the national anthem.

FIRST REPORTER: God forbid! You're right. I can't see any sense

---

° The most influential newspaper in Vienna.
† Location of the Foreign Ministry.
‡ Moriz Benedikt, chief editor and co-owner of the *Neue Freie Presse*.

in our sticking around either. I don't see why, it's only a waste of time. We should be writing about it, instead we're just standing around. By the way, it's very important to describe the people's firm resolve and how here and there somebody separates himself from the crowd to make a donation. You can make a great story out of that. Yesterday he called me in and said we had to stimulate the people's appetite for war—and for the newspaper too—both can be done at the same time. The details are very important, you know, the nuances—and especially the Viennese flavor. For example you have to mention that as a matter of course all class distinctions have been cast aside, and immediately at that. They waved from automobiles, even from horse-drawn carriages. I saw a lady in a lace gown stepping out of her car and hugging a woman with a faded kerchief on her head. It's been that way ever since the ultimatum. Everybody of one heart and one mind.

COACHMAN'S VOICE: Drive on, you damn rascal.

SECOND REPORTER: You know what I've observed? I've noticed how groups have been forming.

FIRST REPORTER: Well?

SECOND REPORTER: And a student made a speech about how everybody must do his duty.

FIRST REPORTER: I can only state that a mood of utmost earnestness is spreading all over the city, and this earnestness, relieved by high spirits and an awareness of experiencing a historical moment, is expressed in every countenance: in those of the men already called to the colors and of those who for the time being are staying home—

VOICE: Kiss my ass!

FIRST REPORTER: —and in the countenance of those privileged to share in this exalted task. Gone is the easygoing nonchalance, the hedonistic thoughtlessness. The keynote now is proud dignity and the confrontation of fate with cheerful earnestness. The physiognomy of our city has changed suddenly. Nowhere is there a trace of uneasiness or gloominess, nowhere fidgety nervousness or troubled minds sicklied o'er with the pale cast of thought. But neither is there frivolous underestimation of the event or foolish, unthinking chauvinism.

CROWD: Hurrah, a German! Down with Serbia!

FIRST REPORTER: Look here, Mediterranean temperament controlled and held in check by German earnestness.

(*Scene change.*)

SCENE 4

The Optimist and the Grumbler conversing.

OPTIMIST: You can consider yourself lucky. In Styria, a Red Cross nurse was shot to death because her car kept rolling a few more feet.

GRUMBLER: The slave has been given power. It won't agree with him.

OPTIMIST: In times of war, regrettably, sometimes the lower echelons unavoidably exceed their authority. But in times such as these all other considerations must be subordinated to one thought—to be victorious!

GRUMBLER: The power that's been given to the slave won't suffice to cope with the enemy—but it will be enough to destroy the state.

OPTIMIST: Militarism means increasing the state's authority by exercising force, so that—

GRUMBLER: —the means will lead to its eventual disintegration, the dissolution of the state. In wartime, everybody becomes his fellow man's superior. The military men become the superiors of the state, which sees no way out of this unnatural constraint but corruption. If the statesman allows the military man to control him, he has fallen under the spell of a grade-school idol which has had its day and which, in our day, can be allowed to rule over life and death only at our peril.

OPTIMIST: I don't see that your gloomy predictions are justified. Just as you did in peacetime, you are obviously drawing overall conclusions from unavoidable accompanying symptoms. You're starting from accidental nuisances, and making them out to be symptomatic. Our time is far too great to bother with trifles.

GRUMBLER: The trifles will grow with the times!

OPTIMIST: This knowledge, that we are living in an era of such tremendous events, will prompt even the most limited among us to rise above themselves.

GRUMBLER: The small thieves who have not yet been hanged will grow up to be big thieves—and then they will get off scot-free.*

OPTIMIST: What even the most insignificant among us will gain from the war is—

GRUMBLER: Filth.

OPTIMIST: Yes, you—you who have seen filth in everything, must now sense that your time is up! Go right on grumbling in your corner as you've always done—the rest of us are marching onward into an era of spiritual uplift! Don't you see that a new time, a time of greatness, has dawned?

---

* Refers to the German proverb: "Small thieves are hanged, the big ones get off scot-free."

GRUMBLER: I knew the time when it was still this small (*gestures*), and it will be small again.

OPTIMIST: Can you be negative even now? Don't you hear this exultation? Don't you see this enthusiasm? Can a feeling heart refuse to abandon itself to it? Only yours could. Do you really think that this mighty emotion of the masses will bear no fruit, that this magnificent beginning will be without a sequel? Those who are rejoicing today—

GRUMBLER: —will be lamenting tomorrow.

OPTIMIST: What does individual sorrow matter? As little as an individual life. Man's vision has at last been raised aloft again. No longer do we live merely for material gain, but also—

GRUMBLER: —for medals.

OPTIMIST: Man does not live by bread alone.

GRUMBLER: He must also make war in order not to have it.

OPTIMIST: There will always be bread! But we live by the hope of final victory, which is not to be doubted, and because of which—

GRUMBLER: —we'll starve to death.

OPTIMIST: Oh, what little faith! How ashamed you will be some day! But don't shut yourself off when there is rejoicing! The soul's gates have been thrown wide open. The memory of these days, in which people back home share in the sufferings and deeds of our glorious frontline fighters—though only by receiving daily war reports—will leave upon the souls of men—

GRUMBLER: —no scars!

OPTIMIST: The people will learn from this war only—

GRUMBLER: —not to refrain from war in the future.

OPTIMIST: The shot is out of the barrel and for mankind—

GRUMBLER: —gone in one ear and out the other!

(*Scene change.*)

SCENE 11

Two Draft Dodgers meet.

FIRST DRAFT DODGER: Well, still in Vienna? Weren't you drafted?

SECOND DRAFT DODGER: I went up and got it fixed. But what are you doing in Vienna? Weren't you drafted?

FIRST DRAFT DODGER: I went up and got it fixed.

SECOND DRAFT DODGER: Of course.

FIRST DRAFT DODGER: Of course.

(*Enter Subscriber to the* Neue Freie Presse *and a Patriot.*)

PATRIOT: Healthy young people. Have you noticed? A whole army corps of them could be put together on the Ringstrasse.

SUBSCRIBER: That's really infuriating. For shame, draft dodgers in France!

PATRIOT: All in all, isn't the sorry state of the enemy countries something? The way things are going!

SUBSCRIBER: You're telling me! Speaking of France, for example, haven't they just announced that they're going to draft rejects? Can you imagine it—drafting rejects!

PATRIOT: As though it weren't enough that they're drafting them; they're even sending them to the front! I read an article on "The Induction of Former Rejects in France."

SUBSCRIBER: And what do you think of the abuses in the French Army Quartermaster Corps?

PATRIOT: War matériel has been contracted at shocking prices.

SUBSCRIBER: Dubious price discrepancies have been reported in purchases of canned goods and ammunition.

PATRIOT: Exorbitant prices have been paid for cloth, linens, and flour.

SUBSCRIBER: Large profits have been realized by certain middlemen! They work with middlemen!

Patriot: Where?

Subscriber: In France, of course.

Patriot: Scandalous.

Subscriber: And this is brought up in open sessions of parliament!

Patriot: As if that would be possible here! Fortunately we have—

Subscriber: No parliament, you mean—

Patriot: No. A clear conscience, I was going to say.

Subscriber: And what about Russia? It's highly significant that they've even had to call the Duma into session. The government must accept being spoken to in plain language.

Patriot: That sort of thing would be out of the question here. Fortunately we have—

Subscriber: A clear conscience, I know.

Patriot: No parliament, I was going to say.

Subscriber: And what do you say to this year's harvest?

Patriot: I can only say: Poor crops in Italy. Crop failure in England. Unfavorable crop prospects in Russia. Uneasiness over crops in France. And what do you say to the exchange rate, eh?

Subscriber: What can I say? The fall of the ruble speaks a language that cannot be misunderstood.

Patriot: Why, if you compare with it our Austrian krone, for example—

Subscriber: The lira's in a bad way, too. It's dropped thirty percent.

Patriot: The krone has only dropped twice that—fortunately. And England. What do you say to that?

Subscriber: I say this: in England potato prices have risen tremendously.

Patriot: Yes. It even turns out that they're lower over there now than they are here in peacetime. Gives you some idea, doesn't it?

SUBSCRIBER: And what about the treatment of our civilian internees? Have you read how they have to suffer? You know how well we're treating the Russian prisoners of war.

PATRIOT: Yes, and in return, of course, they behave with the greatest impudence. I've been told that up in the Brenner Pass in Tyrol we let them dig trenches just to give them something to do. And what do you suppose they do? They refuse. Of course we make short shrift of them. We bring up a firing squad from Innsbruck and then ask them again if they're ready to dig the trenches. No, they say. Rifle at the ready, we say. Why not? Aren't we within our rights? To hell with international law! War's war. But being good-natured, we're still patient and ask them one more time—the rebels. No, they say. Take aim, we say. Then of course —you should have seen them all put their hands up. Yes, they're ready to dig trenches. All of a sudden, let me tell you, they can't wait to dig trenches. That is, all except four of them. Well, those of course were shot. It goes without saying. Among them was a lieutenant—just listen to this—

SUBSCRIBER: I'm listening.

PATRIOT: Probably the ringleader. He had the nerve to stand up and make a speech against Austria. Listen—

SUBSCRIBER: I'm listening.

PATRIOT: Our men—the Austrians, I mean—like the kind-hearted fellows they are, were too excited when it came to firing, and they just couldn't hit them. The captain himself had to take a hand and shot the bastards down with his service revolver. Well, what do you say to the kind of liberties those Russians take with us?

SUBSCRIBER: With us here? Why not talk about the insolent way they treat their Austrian prisoners? In case you haven't read yet what's in today's paper, I've got it right here. Listen to this. "Russian Troops Illegally Force War Prisoners to Participate in Hostilities." From army press headquarters it is reported that, since the Russians were driven out of Galicia, hardly a day has gone by without the disclosure of some hitherto unreported infringement of international law by Russian troops, so that there is hardly a single clause in the Hague Convention that cannot be shown to have been trampled underfoot by the Russians.

PATRIOT: Very good!

SUBSCRIBER: Just listen to this—

PATRIOT: I'm listening.

SUBSCRIBER: Recent police investigations in the formerly occupied areas of Galicia have shown that during the entire occupation, by order of the Russian commanding officers, all able-bodied men and women were, if necessary, in addition to being given other types of work, conscripted specifically for the digging of trenches—

PATRIOT: What do you say to that!

SUBSCRIBER: —for which purpose they were marched as far as the Carpathian Mountains. The Russian authorities are, of course, not troubled by the fact that the enemy is expressly prohibited by the Hague Convention from imposing on the peaceful inhabitants of occupied areas the rendering of services that are in effect directed against their own country.

PATRIOT: Of course, they're not troubled! The bastards!

SUBSCRIBER: Just listen—

PATRIOT: I'm listening.

SUBSCRIBER: It is therefore no small wonder that the Russians, as has similarly been ascertained, are also making improper use of captured members of the Austrian Army in the building of military installations to be used against us—

PATRIOT: Incredible! Exactly the same case!

SUBSCRIBER: —although this too contravenes the clause in the Hague Convention prohibiting prisoners of war from being employed in work that is in any way connected with the war effort.

PATRIOT: That's just like the Russians. Nobody else in the world is like that! And probably none of the poor Austrian soldiers dared to refuse.

SUBSCRIBER: Well, can you imagine the chutzpah of that Russian lieutenant?

PATRIOT: That was an excellent article by Professor Brockhausen, the one in which he said that in this country defenseless war prisoners have never been mocked, not even verbally.

SUBSCRIBER: He was right. That appeared in the paper the same day as the Lemberg City Commandant's statement that Russian prisoners being transported through the streets had been abused and attacked with sticks by a segment of the population. He explicitly stated that such conduct was unworthy of a civilized nation.

PATRIOT: He admitted that we *are* a civilized nation.

SUBSCRIBER: Of course. But there's really no point on which we don't distinguish ourselves from the enemy—who, after all, are nothing but the scum of humanity.

PATRIOT: For example, in the civilized way we speak even when referring to our enemies, who are really the filthiest bastards on God's earth.

SUBSCRIBER: And above all, unlike them, we're always humane. For example, the leading article in the *Presse* shows concern even for the fishes and marine creatures in the Adriatic. These are good days for them, it says, because they're getting so many Italian corpses to feed on. It's really carrying humanitarianism to extremes to think of the fishes and marine creatures in the Adriatic in these callous times when even human beings are going hungry.

PATRIOT: Yes, he sometimes overdoes it. But he really lets them have it. And it's not only in wartime humanitarianism that we're ahead of them, it's also in something else much more valuable: staying power. Over there defeatism is rampant. They'd be glad to see an end to it. Here—

SUBSCRIBER: Yes, I've noticed that too. For instance, there's discouragement in France.

PATRIOT: Listlessness in England.

SUBSCRIBER: Despair in Russia.

PATRIOT: Contrition in Italy.

SUBSCRIBER: In fact, the moods in the Allied countries in general—

PATRIOT: The walls are crumbling.

SUBSCRIBER: Worry is gnawing at Poincaré.

PATRIOT: Grey's down in the mouth.

SUBSCRIBER: The Tsar tosses and turns in bed at night.

PATRIOT: Anguish in Belgium.

SUBSCRIBER: That's a relief! Demoralization in Serbia.

PATRIOT: That makes one feel good! Despair in Montenegro.

SUBSCRIBER: We can take courage! Consternation among the Allies.

PATRIOT: What a lift that gives one! Misgivings in London, Paris, and Rome. Really, you have only to look at the head-lines. There's no need to read any further, since the situation is immediately apparent. You see how badly things are going for them and how well we're doing. We have moods, too, but of a different kind, thank God!

SUBSCRIBER: With us there is joy, confidence, jubilation, hope, and satisfaction. We're always in good spirits, why shouldn't we be? We have every reason to be.

PATRIOT: Sticking it out, for example—we revel in it.

SUBSCRIBER: There's nobody as good at it as we are.

PATRIOT: The Viennese is an especially first-rate stick-it-outer. People here put up with all their hardships as if they were pleasures!

SUBSCRIBER: Hardships? What hardships?

PATRIOT: I mean, if there were any hardships.

SUBSCRIBER: Unfortunately there aren't any!

PATRIOT: That's right. There aren't any. But tell me this—if people have no hardships—why do they have to stick it out?

SUBSCRIBER: I can explain that. There are in fact no hardships, but we take them joyfully in our stride. That's the trick of it. We have always done that well.

PATRIOT: That's right. Standing in line, for example, is great fun. People practically stand in line just to stand in line.

SUBSCRIBER: The only difference between now and before is that now there's a war on. If it weren't for the war, you'd really think it was peacetime. But war is war, and now you *have* to do a lot of things you only *wanted* to do before.

PATRIOT: Precisely. Nothing's changed here. And if they do reexamine the army rejects once in a great while, you really ought to see these men. They just can't wait to get to the front—our boys up to fifty.

SUBSCRIBER: The higher age brackets haven't even been called up yet.

PATRIOT: Did you see this? "Nineteen-Year-Olds Drafted in Italy." The headline alone tells the whole shocking truth.

SUBSCRIBER: No, I must have missed that. What do you say! Such youngsters! In Austria they have to be a bit more mature than that. If I'm not mistaken, we're calling up the fifty-year-olds—only for noncombat zones of course. There are still plenty of forty-nine-year-olds at the front.

PATRIOT: In France they're already up to the forty-eight-year-olds.

SUBSCRIBER: Men with gray hair! All the younger ones seem to have been called up already. In March we're going to trot out our seventeen-year-olds. That will really be a joy.

PATRIOT: Surely, those are the best years. Do you know what also makes the difference? Equipment. For that's the main thing. With us this is simply a matter of course. We don't make any fuss about that. Did you see in today's paper:

"Italians Worried about Warm Mountain Clothing for the Troops"?

SUBSCRIBER: The things they worry about!

PATRIOT: Here we don't fret over things of that sort. Nothing to it! You place the order with the army contractor and that's all there is to it. You've heard the story of the wool blankets, haven't you?

SUBSCRIBER: No.

PATRIOT: There you have an excellent example of the way everything works itself out in this country. Feiner and Company signed a contract with Germany for a million and a half wool blankets. That's about the number our War Ministry thought they were going to need for the Carpathian Mountains this winter. But the Ministry didn't take the matter too seriously since they were counting on final victory long before then. But when the situation got really serious after all, the word went out, all right, but first the customs formalities had to be complied with. The Minister of Finance couldn't be induced to release the goods until that was done, even though the Minister of War insisted that the wool blankets were needed. What can I say—the problem was shunted back and forth between the War Ministry and the Finance Ministry for six months, all through the battle for the Carpathian Mountains. Then the firm got into the act, and Katzenellenbogen from Berlin—you know, our troubleshooter, especially in dealing with the War Ministry —stepped in personally. He went up to see the Minister of Finance and told him to his face that it couldn't be done. The Minister of Finance said he couldn't settle this problem on the spot. So Katzenellenbogen, forceful as he is, you know his energy, well, Katzenbellenbogen told him first that the firm was going bankrupt and second that the wool blankets were rotting. They were lying outdoors in the rain and the cold, and all of them had just about had it.

SUBSCRIBER: All of whom?

PATRIOT: The wool blankets, of course, because they were being kept outdoors.

SUBSCRIBER: Who?

PATRIOT: The blankets of course. Why are you asking? So he told him categorically first that the company was going bankrupt, second that the blankets were rotting, and thirdly, after all, the soldiers needed them. The Minister of Finance shrugged his shoulders and said he couldn't do anything. The file had to be finished first. First the customs duty, then the blankets.

SUBSCRIBER: So why didn't the War Ministry pay it?

PATRIOT: What a question! The Minister of War took the position that he couldn't do it. The file had to be processed first.

SUBSCRIBER: The file on the customs duty? Isn't that the Finance Minister's business?

PATRIOT: No, the file on the authorization of funds to pay the duty.

SUBSCRIBER: Oh, I see. Well, and what happened then? I can't wait to—

PATRIOT: What happened then? Katzenellenbogen went back and said straight to his face: Your Excellency, he said, the War Ministry won't give in. Let me tell you something, he said. In business, if a customer can't pay at the moment, but if you check up on him and find out that he's financially sound, then it's customary to give him credit. Your Excellency, I'd like to tell you something. Check up on the War Ministry. You'll find it's all right. Why be close-minded? Give them credit. Well, that made sense to the Minister of Finance. They gave them credit and the blankets were released.

SUBSCRIBER: Well, everything was then in shipshape order after all?

PATRIOT: So far, yes. But by then it was March. Well, what can I tell you? When they pulled out the blankets, they were completely ruined. So they got refugees to stitch them together by twos and finally, when April came round and everything seemed to be going pretty well—though unfortunately the blankets cost twice the price at which they were ordered because all that labor had to be paid for after all, and patching a million and a half blankets together is no joke—well, by the time they'd got them all done, what do you suppose came to light?

SUBSCRIBER: What?

PATRIOT: It turned out that the soldiers didn't need the blankets any longer. In the first place it was no longer so cold in the Carpathian Mountains by then, and in any case most of the men already had frostbitten feet, anyway. Now, I ask you: do we worry about blankets?

SUBSCRIBER: The Italians do. Serves them right. What do you say to the rise in food prices in Italy?

PATRIOT: I haven't read anything about that. I only read about a poor harvest in Italy.

SUBSCRIBER: Aren't you confusing that with the crop failure in England?

PATRIOT: That's another story, and it has to be distinguished from the food shortage in Russia.

SUBSCRIBER: That's just it. It's the same everywhere. And casualty lists, for example, they have all started publishing them.

PATRIOT: Yes, just as we do here. They copy everything—

SUBSCRIBER: Excuse me. What do you mean by that? Have we—

PATRIOT: On the contrary, here they have now introduced the daily British casualty list.

SUBSCRIBER: I noticed that, too, and I also noticed that our own list appears only once in a blue moon.

PATRIOT: Well, you're not suggesting that we fake lists and invent names for them? At the most we've had maybe eight hundred wounded in the past year.

SUBSCRIBER: In Italy they don't publish any lists at all. That looks more than suspicious. They simply can't admit the hecatombs they've suffered.

PATRIOT: Speaking of Italy, did you see this: "Italian General Relieved of His Command"? For incompetence demonstrated at the front. Further dismissals are imminent.

SUBSCRIBER: Whew! Would you believe that! Have you ever heard of a general in this country—

PATRIOT: Well, actually yes—

SUBSCRIBER: For incompetence?

PATRIOT: For that too!

SUBSCRIBER: But at least he didn't have an opportunity to prove it at the *front*!

PATRIOT: Not that. You're quite right there. By the way, do you know there already are draft dodgers in Italy?

SUBSCRIBER: Where else? And they just got into the war! But do you know what else they've introduced? Censorship. By the way, so far as freedom of opinion is concerned, they're all in a bad way. I've been told that you don't dare open your mouth over there.

PATRIOT: The most their papers are allowed to say is that our military position is a lot better than their own. Oh well, the truth simply can't be suppressed. The British military analysts describe the situation of the Allies as hopeless.

SUBSCRIBER: What are things coming to when they permit that? Whatever would happen to anyone who said that sort of thing here?

PATRIOT: If he said that the situation of the Allies was hopeless?

SUBSCRIBER: No, if he said that the situation of the Central Powers was hopeless. He'd be hanged—and quite rightly, too. No one here would have that nerve.

PATRIOT: Why should he anyhow? He'd be lying. There you are! Even in England they do tell the truth—that is, when they are forced to admit that things are going badly.

SUBSCRIBER: Fine patriots they must be there! Recently some-one over there wrote that Britain deserves to be annihilated by Germany. He really had to pay for that. Do you know how long he got? Fourteen days!

PATRIOT (*clutching his head*): Imprisonment for criticism in England! How do you like that? Fourteen days!

SUBSCRIBER: No, the fine English gentlemen certainly don't like that kind of talk. They can't take the truth. But then no journalist in this country would ever let himself get carried away like that.

PATRIOT: And are things any better in France? Not the least bit. Didn't you see this in today's paper: "Imprisonment for Disseminating the Truth in France"? Now really! Just be-cause someone told the truth. A lady in fact—she said Germany was prepared for war but France wasn't. So if you tell the honest truth to their face for once—

SUBSCRIBER: No. Those who are in power in France can't take that. Waging war, yes. They like that well enough. Attacking Germany, their peaceful neighbor, out of the blue—that's what they like.

PATRIOT: Golden words. Germany is waging a defensive war. Not a living soul in Germany was prepared for war. The big industrialists were virtually stunned.

SUBSCRIBER: That goes without saying. And when that poor soul in France told such a simple truth in plain words that even a layman can understand—

PATRIOT: Just a minute, you've got that wrong. The woman was convicted because she—

SUBSCRIBER: Well, because she told the truth!

PATRIOT: Yes, but after all she did say that Germany *was* prepared for war—

SUBSCRIBER: But the truth is that Germany was *not* prepared for war.

PATRIOT: Yes, but she said Germany *was* prepared for war.

SUBSCRIBER: But that's a lie.

PATRIOT: But she was convicted because she spoke the truth—

SUBSCRIBER: Well, why was she convicted?

PATRIOT: Well, because she said Germany *was* prepared for war.

SUBSCRIBER: But how can she be convicted for that in France? For that she should be convicted in Germany.

PATRIOT: How's that again? Just a minute. No. Or—yes— listen, this is how I explain the matter to myself. She did tell the truth, of course, but in France—you know what they're like over there—she was convicted because she had lied.

SUBSCRIBER: Just a minute. You're all mixed up. I think it's more like this—she had lied and they convicted her because in France they can't take the truth.

PATRIOT: That's it! That's the way it must have been. After all, it's in their blood. Over there people let themselves get carried away and say things—

SUBSCRIBER: Of course. You can read how they tell their government the truth in the newspapers over there and the pack of lies they tell about us. That's perversity! If you believed what the London press writes about us you'd think Britain was done for.

PATRIOT: But look, who believes it? Here people just don't see things that way. The mentality, I've been told, is totally different over there. Thank God! Our newspaper editors— you can safely say that—show even more patriotic spirit than our soldiers.

SUBSCRIBER: By the way, do you know who's going to come here today? Guess! The greatest living writer, Hans Müller.

PATRIOT: No! You can tell Hans Müller from me that he writes exactly what's in my heart. What's he like personally? That interests me. The words that can describe his style are *sunny* and *sweet*. The way he gave that serviceman a kiss right there in the street in Berlin—sweet is not the word for it. And then the prayer in church at the end of his column calling on God to bless our allied arms! He's my special favorite. Of all those who write about the war, none of them, not even Roda Roda or Felix Salten, catches the shoulder-to-shoulder spirit as he does. When he first started his frontline column "Cassianus in the Trenches," it was so genuine, so enthusiastic, one really believed he was out there at the front. Only later I learned by sheer chance that he was in Vienna. He even wrote it right here in Vienna! The way he brings it off! Talented! I'd love to know what he's like personally.

SUBSCRIBER: Personally—that's hard to say. At the moment he's very worried. The day after tomorrow he has to report for his army physical. Poor fellow.

PATRIOT: Oh? And how come he's worried?

SUBSCRIBER: Well, about the physical.

PATRIOT: Worried? Because he's afraid they may not take him?

SUBSCRIBER: I don't understand you. He's worried, of course, because he's afraid they *will* take him.

PATRIOT: Oh, don't kid me! Hans Müller? The Hans Müller who would let himself be torn to bits for the fatherland? You don't say so! I've never heard of any other man about whom you felt so sure he would live and die for the Nibelung troth. On the contrary, I thought that was why he came back from Germany, because he couldn't wait, because he wanted to volunteer. He'd be on top of the world, I thought, if they took him—and ready to kill himself if they didn't.

SUBSCRIBER: Why? You heard yourself that the frontline column came out of Vienna. Just that impressed you—how he managed to write from the front lines right here in Vienna.

PATRIOT: I thought he wrote his frontline column because his feelings were wounded at being rejected—just to show them. He wanted to prove to them the kind of frontline writing he'd be capable of if he really was at the front. I can't believe what you're telling me. You must be confusing him with somebody else.

SUBSCRIBER: He'd be happy if they confused him with somebody else during the physical day after tomorrow.

PATRIOT: Listen, this is really annoying! I can only think that you're not properly informed. Anyone who has written the way Hans Müller has written—so genuinely, so enthusiastically—is bound to be happy to be taken.

SUBSCRIBER (*agitated*): Well then, must they take everybody? Must everybody be happy? May a person have no other worries? Isn't it enough that he's enthusiastic? No, he's got to serve in the army, too! Müller of all people! What a soft heart you have! It's as though you can't wait to see him drill. But you're worrying unnecessarily, and let's hope he is, too. And if they do take him—fortunately Hans Müller has a reputation today. They'll use him as his talents deserve.

(*Scene change.*)

SCENE 26

Southwestern front. A command post on a mountain-top more than fifteen hundred meters high. The table is decorated with flowers and war trophies.

OBSERVER: Here they come now.

SCHALEK° (*at the head of a group of war correspondents*): I see they made preparations to give us a formal reception. Flowers! They are probably meant for my colleagues, and the trophies for me! Thank you, my good men. We've forged ahead to this command post, it doesn't amount to much, but

° Alice Schalek, the first female war correspondent accredited by the Austrian War Ministry.

no matter. We have to be content that it is at least within view of the enemy. Unfortunately, the commander could not grant my ardent request to visit an exposed point, because, he said, it might stir up the enemy.

A RIFLEMAN (*spits and says*): Morning, madam.

SCHALEK: Good Lord, how interesting! There he sits, like a picture, if you didn't know he was alive, you'd say he was painted by Defregger—what am I saying, by Egger-Lienz! It seems to me that he even has a wily, furtive twinkle in his eye! The common man in person! Let me tell you, my good men, what we experienced as we pressed forward to reach you. Well, the road in the valley that's usually so busy is now under the uncontested control of the War Correspondents' Corps. Up on the ridge, I felt, for the very first time, something like satisfaction when I saw a hotel in the Dolomites transformed into military quarters. Where are they now, those painted signorinas fluttering with lace, where is the Italian hotelkeeper? Not a trace of them left! Aaah—makes me feel good! The officer who was our guide had to think for a while which peak might be most suitable for us. He suggested one that was least under enemy fire, my colleagues agreed, of course, but I said, no, I won't go along with that; and so we finally have come up here. That's the least we could do! Now I want you to answer just one question: How is it that before the war I never saw all those splendid figures that I now meet every day? The common man is really a sight worth seeing! In the city—God, how dull! Here, everybody is an unforgettable figure. Where is the officer?

OFFICER (*from within*): Busy.

SCHALEK: That doesn't matter. (*The Officer emerges. She starts drawing tight-lipped responses to her demand for details. She then asks*): Now where is the lookout? You must have a lookout, musn't you? Every place I went, they had a lookout for me in the observer's dugout, two inches wide, between the moss-camouflaged shelter. Ah—there it is! (*She steps up to the observer's lookout.*)

OFFICER (*shouting*): Get your head down! (*She ducks.*) Those guys over there have no way of knowing where we observers are sitting—the tip of a nose could give us away. (*The male war correspondents in the group get out their handkerchiefs and cover their noses.*)

SCHALEK (*aside*): Cowards! (*The guns begin to operate.*) Thank God, we came just in time. Now a show is beginning—now you tell me, lieutenant, whether an artist's art could make this spectacle more gripping, more passionate. Those who stay at home—let them go on calling the war the shame of the century—even I did as long as I was back home—but those who are out here are gripped by the fever of actual experience. Isn't it true, lieutenant, you who are right in the midst of the war, you might as well admit it, that many of you wouldn't even want the war to end!

(*The sound of hissing projectiles is heard overhead.*)

SCHALEK: Sss! That was a shell.

OFFICER: No, that was shrapnel. Don't you know the difference?

SCHALEK: Apparently it's difficult for you to understand that my ears do not yet separate the finer sound nuances. But I have learned so much since I have been out here, I'll learn that too. —It seems the show is over. What a pity—it was first-rate!

OFFICER: Are you satisfied?

SCHALEK: Satisfied? Satisfied is not the word for it! Patriotism, you idealists may call it. Hatred of the enemy, you nationalists. Call it sport, you moderns. Adventure, you romantics. You who know the souls of men call it the joyous thrill of power. I call it humanity liberated.

OFFICER: What do you call it?

SCHALEK: Humanity liberated.

OFFICER: Yeah—if you could only get a furlough, once in a blue moon!

SCHALEK: But for that you are compensated by deadly peril every hour of the day—that's what I call living! Do you know what interests me most of all? What goes on in your mind, what kind of sentiments do you have? It is amazing how easily men at an altitude of fifteen hundred meters can get by not just without women's help, but without us women altogether.

A RUNNER (*enters*): Beg to report, sir, Sergeant Hofer is dead.

SCHALEK: How simply the simple man makes his report! He is white as a sheet. Call it patriotism, hatred of the enemy, sport, adventure, or the joyous thrill of power—*I* call it humanity liberated. I am gripped by the fever of this experience! Lieutenant, just tell me now, what goes on in your mind, what do you feel?

(*Scene change.*)

SCENE 28

In the chief editor's office. The voice of Benedikt as he dictates.

And the fishes, lobsters, and sea spiders of the Adriatic have for a long time not had it so good as now. In the southern Adriatic they helped themselves to the crew of the *Leon Gambetta* almost to the last man. The dwellers in the mid-Adriatic found nutriment in those Italians whom we could not rescue from the vessel *Turbine*. In the northern Adriatic the creatures of the sea are feasting at an ever more abundant table. The armored cruiser *Amalfi* has joined the *Medusa* and the two torpedo boats. The sample collection of maritime booty, which so far has been limited to maritime small craft, has been significantly augmented. And more bitter than ever must be the taste of the Adriatic, whose

bottom is covered more and more with broken hulks of
Italian ships. And over its blue waters wafts the decomposi-
tion of the fallen liberators of the Karst plateau.

(*Scene change.*)

SCENE 29

The Optimist and the Grumbler conversing.

OPTIMIST: You cannot deny that the war, aside from the
way it fortifies those who constantly have to look death in
the eye, has also brought with it a spiritual uplift.

GRUMBLER: I don't envy death now that so many poor devils
have to look into his eyes; these are men who are elevated
to a metaphysical level only by the universal gallows duty,
and even then not always.

OPTIMIST: The good become better and the bad become good.
War purifies.

GRUMBLER: It deprives the good of their faith, if not of their
lives, and it makes the bad worse. The contrasts of peacetime were great enough.

OPTIMIST: Do you perhaps want to deny the enthusiasm
with which our brave soldiers go into the field, and the
pride with which those remaining at home follow them with
their eyes?

GRUMBLER: Certainly not; I only contend that our brave soldiers would sooner change places with those proudly following them with their eyes than those proudly following
them with their eyes would change places with our brave
soldiers.

OPTIMIST: Do you want to deny the great solidarity that the
war has produced, as if with one magic stroke?

GRUMBLER: The solidarity would be still greater if no one had to march to the front and all might proudly follow with their eyes.

OPTIMIST: The German Kaiser said, "There are no political parties any more; now there are only Germans."

GRUMBLER: That may be right for Germany; but perhaps in other places human beings have a still higher ambition. One should gradually accustom oneself to interpreting what we call British envy, French thirst for revenge, and Russian rapacity as an aversion to the iron tread of sweaty German feet.

OPTIMIST: So you don't believe that it is simply a case of a premeditated surprise attack?

GRUMBLER: But yes! Yes, I do.

OPTIMIST: So how——?

GRUMBLER: As a rule a surprise attack is made against the party who is attacked, less often against the one who attacks. Or let us call it a surprise attack that came as something of a surprise to those attacking, and an act of self-defense that took the attackers a little bit by surprise.

OPTIMIST: You seem to find that funny.

GRUMBLER: In all seriousness, I take this European alliance against central Europe as the last profound effort of which Christian civilization is capable.

OPTIMIST: Thus you are obviously of the opinion that it was not central Europe but rather the allies that acted in self-defense. What if, however, as may happen, they are not capable of successfully carrying through this self-defense of a surprise attack?

GRUMBLER: Then this traders' war will be decided for the present in favor of those who had less religion, in order to change after a hundred years into an outright religious war.

OPTIMIST: How do you mean that?

GRUMBLER: I mean that then the Judaized Christianity of Europe will surrender to the command of the Asiatic spirit.

OPTIMIST: And how would the Asiatic spirit force it to that?

GRUMBLER: With massive quantity and a developed technology by which alone the infernal spirit of central Europe can be gotten the better of. The quantity China already has, the other weapon she will procure for herself in good time. And in time China will see to it that she is Japanized. She will proceed as England, on a smaller scale, is proceeding today, in that she will have to become militaristic in order to take the teeth out of militarism.

OPTIMIST: But England is not keeping militarism within bounds.

GRUMBLER: I hope she does. And that she will not be done in herself, if she succumbs to militarism; and that she will not purchase material victory at the cost of spiritual impoverishment. Otherwise Europe will be Germanized. Militarism is perhaps a system by which a European people is conquered after it has conquered through it. The Germans had to be the first to give up their better selves in order to be the most powerful military nation on earth. Let's hope that the same doesn't happen to others, especially the English, who until now have been saved from compulsory military service by a nobler drive for self-preservation. The present self-defense, which demands general conscription, is only a desperate measure of dubious success. England could defeat itself in the process of defeating Germany. The only race strong enough to survive the technological life does not live in Europe. That's the way I see it at times. May the Christian God grant that it be otherwise!

OPTIMIST: Aha, your Chinese, the race most unfit for war!

GRUMBLER: Certainly, today they lack all the achievements of modern times, for perhaps in a remote era unknown to us they already lived through them and have managed to preserve their inner lives. They will easily attain these achievements again as soon as they need them in order to disabuse Europeans of them. They will also deal in military tomfoolery, but to a moral purpose. That's what I call my kind of religious war that has character.

OPTIMIST: What idea will it help triumph?

GRUMBLER: The idea that God created man not as consumer or producer but rather as human being. That the means of life should not be the goal of life. That the stomach should not outgrow the head. That life is not exclusively based upon the profit motive. That the human being is allotted time in order to have time and not to arrive somewhere faster with his legs than with his heart. What is alive in the instinct of even the most enslaved mankind, is its longing to protect the freedom of the spirit against the dictatorship of money, to protect human dignity against the autocracy of acquisitiveness.

OPTIMIST: The Germans are after all also the people of poets and thinkers. Does German education not contradict the materialism that you allege?

GRUMBLER: German education has no content, but is merely a house decoration with which the people of judges and hangmen ornament their emptiness.

OPTIMIST: The people of judges and hangmen? You call them that? The people of Goethe and Schopenhauer?

GRUMBLER: Goethe and Schopenhauer would, with more justice and severity than *Le Matin* does, reproach today's Germans with everything that they had in their hearts against their own German contemporaries. Today they would be lucky if, as undesirable nonaliens, they were fortunate enough to escape over the border. Goethe was able to derive nothing but the feeling of emptiness from the emotionally exalted state of his people during the wars of liberation. We would be fortunate if colloquial and journalistic German were still at the level at which Schopenhauer found it contemptible. No people lives further from its language, thus from the source of its life, than the Germans. What Neapolitan beggar is not closer to his language than the German professor to his! Yes, but this people is more educated than any other, and since without exception its Ph.D.'s—unless they've managed to get into the press corps—know how to handle gas bombs, it rushes to give its field commanders Ph.D.'s. What would Schopenhauer have said to a faculty of philosophy that awards its highest honor to an organizer of mechanical death? Educated they are; British envy has got to concede that to them, and they know everything there is to know about everything. Their language is merely good enough to meet primitive needs. Today people write the stunted artificial pidgin language of sales jargon and abandon their classics to the pitiless barbarism of the hucksters. At a time when no human being divines and feels the soul of words any more, the German people find compensation in deluxe printings, bibliophily, and similar obscenities of an aestheticism that is as genuine a stigma of barbarism as is the bombardment of a cathedral.

OPTIMIST: But I don't quite understand what you are saying about the German language. After all, you're the one who acts as if you were betrothed to the German language and, in your treatise against Heine you claimed its superiority over the Romance languages. Now you evidently think differently.

GRUMBLER: Only a German would find that I think differently now. It is precisely because I am betrothed to her that I think this way. I am also faithful to her. And I know that a victory, which God may spare us, would be the most complete betrayal of man's spiritual nature.

OPTIMIST: But you do see the German language as the more deeply profound?

GRUMBLER: Yes, but far beneath its level are those who speak it.

OPTIMIST: And in your opinion don't the other languages rank far below the German language?

GRUMBLER: Yes, but those who speak them rank far above.

OPTIMIST: Are you then in a position to establish a tangible connection between language and the war?

GRUMBLER: Yes: those who speak a language that is the most congealed into set phrases and stock terminology have the tendency and the readiness to find, in accents of conviction, blameless in themselves everything that they find blameworthy in others.

OPTIMIST: And is this supposed to be a quality of the German language?

GRUMBLER: For the most part yes. The language itself is now a manufactured product like other products whose sale absorbs the lives of those who speak German today.

OPTIMIST: And aren't the others also out for business?

GRUMBLER: But their lives aren't swallowed up by it.

OPTIMIST: The English make a business of war and have always had only mercenaries do their fighting for them.

GRUMBLER: That's because the English are not idealists; they don't want to stake their lives on their business.

OPTIMIST: But our soldiers are fighting for the fatherland.

GRUMBLER: Yes, they really are, and luckily, they're doing it with willing enthusiasm, because otherwise they would be forced to do it. The English are no idealists. They are so honest that, if they want to do business, they don't call it fatherland; they are said not even to have a word for it in their language; they don't drag in ideals when the export market is in danger.

OPTIMIST: They are traders.

GRUMBLER: And we are heroes. They don't want to be forced by any cutthroat competitors to work longer than six hours because they want to reserve the rest of the day for those interests for which God created the British—God or sport. The interest in God is a turning away from the world of commerce even if only hypocritically, because at any rate it's an idea that leads far away from daily labor. And that is the important thing. In contrast to this, the German works twenty-four hours a day. By applying to his daily work— as an ornament, as a trademark, as packaging—aspects of his spiritual, intellectual, artistic, and other concerns, he fulfills all those obligations that he would neglect if he had to attend to each separately. He doesn't want to pass anything up. And this mixture of inner things with the necessities of life—this is the unfortunate element in which German genius flowers and fades.

OPTIMIST: The cause of the war, as everybody knows, is that Germany wanted to have her place in the sun.

GRUMBLER: That is well known, but people don't yet know that, if this place is indeed won, the sun will go down. As a grumbler, I am obliged to look at the dark side of everything and to fear that that nation will be victorious that has preserved the least individuality—in other words, the Germans. However, mostly I'm an optimist, but of a kind quite different from you. And when I am, I hope with confidence that it will come out well, and I realize that all these victories are nothing but a wanton loss of time and blood for the sake of postponing the inevitable defeat. I fear our victory and hope for our defeat. In the past, war was a tournament of the few, and now it involves the multitude. It used to be a contest between the strong, now it is a battle of machines.

OPTIMIST: The development of weapons cannot possibly lag behind the technical achievements of modern times.

GRUMBLER: No, but the imagination of modern times has lagged behind the technical achievements of mankind.

OPTIMIST: Yes, but does one wage war by imagination?

GRUMBLER: No, for if we still had imagination, we would no longer wage war.

OPTIMIST: Why not?

GRUMBLER: Because then the stimulus of a phraseology left over from a decrepit ideal would not befog our brains. Because we would be able to imagine even the most unimaginable horror and would anticipate how quickly the road is traversed from the colorful phrases and all the flags of enthusiasm to the field-gray* of misery. Because the prospect of dying of dysentery for the fatherland or of having one's feet get frostbitten would no longer set ringing oratory into motion. Because we would at least know with certainty that in setting out for the front we would get full of lice for the fatherland. And because we would know that man has invented the machine only to be overpowered by it, and because we would not outdo the madness of having invented it with the worse madness of letting ourselves be killed by it. Had we imagination, we would know that it is a crime to expose life to chance, and a sin to degrade death to chance. That it is folly to build armored ships if one builds torpedo boats to outwit them. Folly, to make mortars if, as a defense against them, one digs trenches in which only the man who first sticks his head out is lost. Folly, to chase mankind into mouseholes, in flight before his own weapons, and henceforth to let mankind enjoy peace only under the earth. If we had imagination instead of newspapers, then technology would not be the means for making life harder, and science would not strive to annihilate life.

---

* The color of the front-line uniform.

OPTIMIST: But when you speak of a war of multitudes, aren't you demonstrating your own conviction about the necessity of war itself? For you thus admit that for a time war will also solve the problem of overpopulation.

GRUMBLER: That it does thoroughly. Concern about overpopulation might give way to concern about depopulation. The legalization of abortion would have eliminated those concerns more painlessly than a world war, without bringing it on.

OPTIMIST: Prevailing moral opinion would never consent to that!

GRUMBLER: I never thought it would, since prevailing moral opinion only consents to having fathers—whom chance had not been able to kill off—slink through the world as starving cripples and mothers bear children for aerial bombs to tear apart. With regret and yet it happens. Rather rich experience in this area could have brought those who order murder from the air, and those who are entrusted with its execution, to the final awareness that although their intention is to hit an arsenal, they must unavoidably hit a bedroom instead, and in place of a munitions factory, a girls' school. Repeated experience should have taught them that this is the result of those attacks they afterward boastingly recall as a successful bombing mission.

OPTIMIST: All in all, it is a permissible means of war, and now that man has conquered the skies—

GRUMBLER: —the scoundrel immediately uses the opportunity to make the earth unsafe, too. Read the description of the ascent in a balloon in Jean Paul's *Kampanertal*. These five pages could no longer be written today because the guest of the air no longer cherishes a veneration for the heavens —instead, an intruder into the air, he uses the safe distance from the earth to assault it. Man takes revenge on himself for any progress he makes. He immediately employs against

life precisely those things that should sustain life. He makes
it difficult for himself with just those things that should
make life easier. Ascent in an air balloon is an act of devotion; ascent in an airplane is a danger for those who are
not on board.

OPTIMIST: But surely also for the bomb-dropping flyer himself.

GRUMBLER: Oh, yes, but not the danger of being killed by
those whom he will kill, and he can more easily elude the
machine guns that lie in wait than the defenseless ones
below can elude him. He also more easily eludes the honest
combat between two equally armed murderers: honest, insofar as the desecration of the element in which it takes
place admits this evaluation. The aerial bomb, however, is
always—even if "the courageous one" handles it—the arm-
ing of cowardice; it is as wicked as the U-boat, which
demonstrates the principle of armed perfidy, that kind of
perfidy that lets the dwarf triumph over the armed giant.
The infants whom the flyer kills are, however, not armed,
and even if they were, they would hardly be able to reach
the flyer as unfailingly as he can reach them. The greatest
disgrace of this war is that the single invention that brought
mankind closer to the stars has served solely to prove
his earthly wretchedness even in the air, as if it weren't
sufficiently widespread on earth.

OPTIMIST: And the infants who are starved?

GRUMBLER: The governments of the Central Powers have the
option of saving their infants from this fate by weaning
their adults from their patriotic primers. Even assuming
that enemy rulers share equal guilt with our own for the
blockade, the bombardment of enemy infants as reprisal
represents a notion that does all honor to German ideology,
an intellectual shelter, in which I, by the German God,
would not like to live!

OPTIMIST: It cuts me to the quick to hear you speak this way

—but this really means that you insist on seeing as small, a time that must appear great to even the most nearsighted. May God grant you larger ideas. Perhaps they will come to you tomorrow during Mozart's "Requiem." Come with me, the net proceeds go to the War Assistance Fund—

GRUMBLER: No, the poster is enough for me—but what sort of strange drawing is that? A church window? If my nearsightedness doesn't deceive me—a mortar! Is it possible? Yes, who has succeeded in reconciling both worlds? Mozart and mortar! What a concert arrangement! Who has made such a felicitous combination? No, one must not weep about it. Only tell me, would such a betrayal of God be possible even in the culture of the Senegal Negro, whom the enemy has called in to help against us?

OPTIMIST (*after a pause*): I think you are right. But God knows, only you see it that way. It eludes the likes of us, and therefore we see the future in a rosy light. You see it, and therefore it is there. Your mind's eye invokes it and then your eyes see it.

GRUMBLER: Because they are nearsighted. They perceive the contours and imagination does the rest. And my ear hears noises that others don't hear, and these noises disturb the music of the spheres for me, something else others don't hear. Think that over, and then if you still don't come to a conclusion by yourself, call me. I like to converse with you, you supply the key words for my monologues. I would like to go before the public with you. As of now I can only say to them that I am remaining silent, and if possible, what I am remaining silent about.

OPTIMIST: What for instance?

GRUMBLER: For instance: That this war, if it doesn't kill the good, may perhaps create a moral island for the good, who were good even without it. That the war, however, will transform the whole surrounding world into a great rear-guard of deceit, debility, and the most inhuman betrayal of God, in that evil keeps working on beyond the war and because of it, becoming fat behind pretended ideals and waxing on sacrifice! That in this war, the war of today, culture does not renew itself, but rather saves itself from the hangman by committing suicide. That the war has been more than sin; that it has been a lie, a daily lie, out of which printer's ink flowed like blood, the one nourishing the other, streaming out in several directions, a delta toward the great sea of insanity. That this war should be ended not by peace, but rather by a war of the cosmos against this rabid planet!

OPTIMIST: You are an optimist. You believe and hope that the world is coming to an end.

GRUMBLER: No, it is only running its course like my night-mare, and when I die, it will all be over. Sleep well!

(*Exit.*)

Act II

SCENE 10

The Optimist and the Grumbler conversing.

OPTIMIST: One thing, at any rate, I can affirm with a clear conscience: Since the declaration of war I have not met so much as one young man in Vienna, who was still there, and if he was still there, was not feverishly impatient not to be there any longer.

GRUMBLER: I don't get around much. But my phone is on a party line. Before the war I could listen in on every conversation in the area—about a poker game setup, a prospective business deal, and some eagerly desired sex. I could do all this effortlessly, without so much as having to ring for the operator. My sole connections with the outside world are the wrong ones. Ever since the outbreak of the war, which has in no way improved the national telephone service, the conversations concern yet another problem, and every single day, whenever I am called to the telephone to listen to other people talk to each other, which is at least ten times every day, I hear conversations such as these: "Gus went up and got things fixed." "And how is Rudi doing?" "Rudi went up, too, and he also got things fixed." "And what about Pepi? Has he already gone off to the front by any chance?" "Pepi has lumbago. But as soon as he can get out of bed he, too, is going to go up and get things fixed."

OPTIMIST: Watch your words.

GRUMBLER: Why? I could prove it.

OPTIMIST: From your point of view you ought to welcome the getting away of each and every one.

GRUMBLER: Yes, every single one. If I consider the compulsion to die a disgrace, privileged treatment in the face of death merely sharpens the disgrace into feeling that only as a suicide can one go on living in this country.

OPTIMIST: But there have to be exceptions, after all. Literature, for instance. The fatherland needs not only soldiers—

GRUMBLER: —but also lyric poets who give them the courage which they themselves do not possess.

OPTIMIST: But the higher purpose has most decidedly made our poets grow. You cannot possibly deny that they, too, have been steeled by the war.

GRUMBLER: In most of them, it has mobilized the greed for profit, in the few with character, only their stupidity.

OPTIMIST: Ah, yes, in times such as these all poets are swept along—

GRUMBLER: —to sing the deeds of those who desecrate creation.

OPTIMIST: Look at Kernstock—

GRUMBLER: I'd rather not.

OPTIMIST: A poet of Christian mildness, a religious man even by profession.

GRUMBLER: Yes, I admit, he has been steeled to an extraordinary degree. I am thinking in particular of the verses with which he exhorts his Styrian lads to squeeze blood-red wine from Dagos and Frogs.

OPTIMIST: Or think of Brother Willram—

GRUMBLER: Unfortunately my memory doesn't fail me. Isn't he the Christian poet to whom blood is a red flowering and who dreams of a springtime of blood.

OPTIMIST: In every country the church implores God to bestow His blessing upon the weapons of its own people—

GRUMBLER: —and strives to increase them still further. Admittedly we cannot expect the church to implore God to bestow His blessings upon the weapons of the enemy, but it could at least have brought itself to curse its own. Then the churches of the warring nations would have understood each other better. Now it is possible that the Pope deplores the war but speaks of "rightful national aspirations," and that on the very same day the Archbishop of Vienna blesses the war that is being waged as a defense against "ruthless national aspirations." Yes, if inspiration had been stronger than the aspirations, these would not exist—and neither would the war.

OPTIMIST: It's just that the international of the churches was a still greater failure than the red international.

GRUMBLER: The only international that has proved itself is the press . . .

OPTIMIST: It is gratifying to see that you recognize its power—

GRUMBLER: What is a Benedict against—

OPTIMIST: What do you have against—

GRUMBLER: But I am speaking of the Pope. What can a sermon in favor of peace accomplish against an editorial in favor of the war. And since all sermons are in favor of the war—

OPTIMIST: I'll admit that. In Bethlehem the world's salvation was decided in another manner.

GRUMBLER: Bethlehem in America is correcting the mistake that was made nineteen centuries ago.

OPTIMIST: In America? What do you mean?

GRUMBLER: Bethlehem is the name of the largest cannon foundry in the United States.

OPTIMIST: This then is the name of the place from which Germany's enemies are being supplied with weapons!

GRUMBLER: By Germans.

OPTIMIST: You're joking. Carnegie is at the head of the steel trust.

GRUMBLER: Schwab is at the head.

OPTIMIST: You mean the enemies are now being supplied by German-Americans?

GRUMBLER: By German nationals.

OPTIMIST: Who says so?

GRUMBLER: Those who know. The *Wall Street Journal*, which is supposed to be at least as knowledgeable as our own financial journals, ascertained that twenty percent of the steel trust shares are in German hands, not in German-American hands, but in the hands of German nationals. More than that. Here, why don't you read what a German socialist newspaper says about it: "While it has been learned that several authentic Anglo-American manufacturers have turned down orders from the French and British governments, the socialist *Leader*, published in Milwaukee, has listed the names of several German-Americans who publicly embrace the cause of Germany loudly and zealously—

(*A group of young men with paper lanterns passes, singing the song: "Dear Fatherland, You Need Not Worry."*)

—while the factories they direct produce bullets, rifles, and other war matériel for Britain and France. Yes, and that's not the worst: in the United States branches of native German companies are a party to these transactions! That being the case, does one still have the right to find fault with the strange neutrality of America, which, after all, has no reason to forgo these gigantic profits for the sake of our beautiful eyes?"

OPTIMIST: As far as politics is concerned, I say nothing succeeds like success. For that reason the sinking of the *Lusitania* will make a considerable impression.

GRUMBLER: Such an impression it has indeed made. In the whole world, so far as it is still capable of revulsion. But also in Berlin.

OPTIMIST: Even in Berlin?

GRUMBLER: This can also be proved only by proofs. (*He reads aloud.*) "At the moment the ship went under, hundreds of people jumped into the sea. Most of them were torn away by the eddy. Many held onto pieces of wood torn loose by the explosion . . . in Queenstown tragic things could be observed. Wives were seeking their husbands, mothers calling for their children, middle-aged women roaming about with hair dripping with water, young women aimlessly wandering about, pressing their children to their breasts. One hundred and twenty-six bodies were already lying in a heap, among whom were men, women, and children of every age. Two poor little children held themselves tightly embraced in death. It was a pitiful, unforgettable sight." This should impress you.

OPTIMIST: Well, but as to Berlin?

GRUMBLER: Berlin. In a nightclub on the very day after the catastrophe a film showing all this was offered. The program read: "Poland: the sinking of the *Lusitania*. True to nature. At this time of the program, smoking permitted."

OPTIMIST: That is certainly in bad taste.

GRUMBLER: No, it is in style.

OPTIMIST: Well, I cannot take a sentimental view of the *Lusitania* incident.

GRUMBLER: Nor can I—only criminally.

OPTIMIST: The people were warned.

GRUMBLER: The warning against the danger was the threat of a crime; consequently, the murder was preceded by blackmail. To exonerate himself, the blackmailer can never claim that he had previously threatened to commit the crime he then did commit. If I threaten to kill you in case you refuse to do, or not to do, something on which I have no claim, I am extortioning, not warning. After the deed I am a murderer, not an executioner.

OPTIMIST: The deed was not noble but useful. The *Lusitania* carried weapons on board, weapons that were intended for German soldiers.

GRUMBLER: German weapons.

(*Scene change.*)

SCENE 16

A command office.

A MEMBER OF THE GENERAL STAFF (*entering, goes to the telephone*):—Hello, well, do you have the report on Przemyśl ready?—Not yet? Ah, you're still a little sleepy—well, get at it, or else you'll be late again for the partying. Now listen —what, did you forget it all again? You really are— Listen carefully. Let.me impress on you once more the main points to stress. First of all, the fortress wasn't any good anyway. That's the most important thing—What? You can't—what? You can't make people forget that the fortress had always been the pride—you can make people forget just about everything, my friend! So listen to me, the fortress wasn't any good any more, nothing but an old heap of rubbish—

What do you mean, the most modern artillery? I'm telling you, nothing but an old heap of rubbish, understand? Now then, fine. Secondly, pay attention: Not by enemy power but by hunger, understand? But at the same time don't make too big a thing out of the insufficient supply of provisions, you know what I mean—screen out anything about poor organization, any muddle, as best you can. These explanations suggest themselves, but you'll manage all right. Hunger is the main thing. Pride in hunger, understand! Not because of hunger but because of enemy power—uh, what did I say, not because of force but because of hunger. Now then, that should do it—What? That won't work? Because then they'll realize no provisions—what?—and because then they'll want to know why there weren't enough provisions? Okay, fine, just pretend to agree and say: impossible to store as many provisions as necessary because the enemy gets them anyway when he takes the fortress—How would he have taken it then? By hunger? No, of course not, in that case it would have been enemy power—don't ask so many questions. Don't you understand, if he takes the fortress by force and we have the provisions, then he takes the provisions too. That's why we mustn't have provisions, then he doesn't take the provisions, but he takes the fortress by hunger, but not by force. Now you'll manage all right. So long, now—I have to go to the mess hall. I don't intend to surrender to hunger. That's all!

(*Scene change.*)

SCENE 29

The Optimist and the Grumbler conversing.

OPTIMIST: All right, what then would be your idea of a hero's death?

GRUMBLER: A calamitous act of chance.

OPTIMIST: If the fatherland thought that way, it would be in trouble.

GRUMBLER: The fatherland does think that way.

OPTIMIST: What? It calls a hero's death a calamity? An act of chance?

GRUMBLER: Just about that. The fatherland speaks of it as a "cruel blow of fate."

OPTIMIST: Who? Where? There is no military obituary that does not say it is a privilege for a soldier to die for the fatherland. There's never a death announcement in which even the most unassuming private individual does not proclaim plainly and proudly that his son died a hero's death. Even though under other circumstances that same man would talk about a son's death as a "cruel blow of fate." For instance, look at this in today's *Neue Freie Presse*.

GRUMBLER: I see it. But turn back to this page. Here the Chief of Staff, Conrad von Hötzendorf, thanks the mayor for his condolences "on the occasion of the cruel blow of fate" that fell upon him when his son was killed in the line of duty. He used the same language in the family's announcement of his son's death. You are quite right that every neighborhood shopkeeper whose boy has fallen in action assumes the officially dictated posture of a hero's father. The Chief of Staff renounces the mask and reverts to expressing the plain old-fashioned sentiment that is more justified here than in the face of any other kind of death and that is still alive in this conventional phrase. A Bavarian princess congratulated a relative of hers on the occasion of his son's heroic death. At such social heights there exists a certain obligation to behave like one of the furies. The Chief of Staff not only accepts condolences, but time and again he laments the cruelty of fate. The man who is a bit closer to this kind of fate than the entire cast, that is, closer than the soldiers who may be its victims, closer than the fathers of the soldiers who may lament it, he who is author of this drama of fate, and if not that, its producer, or, let us say, its director, and if not that, at least its stage manager—it is precisely this man who speaks of the cruel blow of fate. And he tells the truth, and all the others are compelled to lie. Stricken by his personal grief, he has discarded the obligation to be heroic and, as is only right, has returned to reality. The others remain imprisoned—they must lie.

OPTIMIST: No! They are not lying. People respond to a hero's death with deeply felt sorrow. The prospect of dying on the field of honor often enraptures the sons of the common folk.

GRUMBLER: Unfortunately it also enraptures the mothers who have renounced their power to save the age from this disgrace.

OPTIMIST: It's just that they have not gotten to the level of your kind of subversive thinking. The fatherland is even further from it. That the top people must think so goes without saying. The incident you mention was an accident. Baron Conrad simply used a conventional phrase. He allowed it to slip out—

GRUMBLER: Yes, his feelings showed.

OPTIMIST: In any case, it proves nothing. Something else I

want to show you proves more—it proves everything about
my point of view. It will be proof even for you—

GRUMBLER: Of what?

OPTIMIST: Of the sheer magical unity of this closing of ranks
in shared sorrow, in which all classes vie with each other—

GRUMBLER: Come to the point!

OPTIMIST: Here it is—just wait. I must read this aloud, so
that I am sure you don't miss a word. "A proclamation of
the Ministry of War. The Telegraph Press Bureau reports:
The Ministry of War of the Austro-Hungarian Monarchy
grants permission for the entire labor force employed by
such plants as are engaged in the production of ammunition
and in the development and production of army supplies
to be given a special holiday on the eighteenth day of
August. The Ministry of War sees fit to use this occasion to
emphasize the extraordinary sense of duty and the inde-
fatigable hard work of all members of the labor force, who
have, through the sweat of their brow, helped our incom-
parably brave soldiers to reap the laurels of glorious victory
in death-defying valor." Well? (*The Grumbler remains
silent.*) You seem to be speechless. The social-democratic
press prints it under the headline: "Workers' Contribution
Acknowledged." Nevertheless, many of these workers may
be unhappy that as their reward they got just a day off, even
if that day is the Emperor's birthday—

GRUMBLER: Surely—

OPTIMIST: —instead of being granted the satisfaction of finally
being taken out of the factory—

GRUMBLER: How true.

OPTIMIST: —and of permitting them the opportunity of using
at the front the ammunition that back here they are merely
called upon to produce. These brave men are certainly in-
consolable because it is only through working with their

hands that they are allowed to manifest their solidarity with their fellow countrymen and class comrades, and not also through joining them in their turn in death-defying bravery. The opportunity of getting to the front, this highest honor that any mortal—

GRUMBLER: Mortality seems to be the primary prerequisite. You believe then that being sent to the front is considered the highest reward—by the recipients?

OPTIMIST: Yes, I do.

GRUMBLER: That may well be so. But do you also believe that it is bestowed as the highest reward?

OPTIMIST: No doubt about that! The matter seems to have left you speechless.

GRUMBLER: It has. And that's why, instead of using my own words, I can reciprocate only by the text of an official proclamation. I shall read it aloud to make sure that no word escapes you.

OPTIMIST: From a newspaper?

GRUMBLER: No! It could hardly be published. In place of it there would be a blank space. But it is displayed in those industrial plants which, enjoying the benefit of having been placed under government protection, have managed to rid themselves of any dissatisfaction in the work force.

OPTIMIST: But you heard yourself that the workers are enthusiastically behind the common effort and that they are at worst dissatisfied because they can contribute in no other way. When even the Ministry of War acknowledges the dedication—

GRUMBLER: Seemingly, you are ready to compensate for my speechlessness by jumping into the breach. Why not give the Ministry of War a chance to have its say. "June 14, 1915. It has come to the attention of the Ministry of War that the conduct of workers in numerous industrial plants which have been requisitioned in accordance with the War Production Law is extremely unsatisfactory in terms of discipline and morale. Insubordination, impertinence, refusal to obey foremen and supervisors, passive resistance, wanton destruction of equipment, unauthorized absence from the place of work, and the like are offenses against which in many cases even criminal prosecution proves ineffectual—"

OPTIMIST: The men are obviously impatient to get to the front. This reward is withheld from them.

GRUMBLER: No, it is offered to them. "For this reason the Ministry of War feels it incumbent upon itself to decree that in such cases penal law must absolutely be invoked. The penalties provided in the present context are severe and can be made more so by appropriate intensification. Furthermore, those found guilty draw no wages while serving their sentences so that in such cases court convictions should be a highly effective deterrent and inducement to reform—"

OPTIMIST: Well yes, those are severe penalties—such individuals have also forfeited the chance of ever being sent to the front.

GRUMBLER: Not quite. "Able-bodied workers of military age who are found to be ringleaders punishable by law shall, after the completion of the court proceedings and after they have served the sentences imposed upon them, not be assigned to the plant. Instead, it shall be incumbent upon the military commander of the plant involved to refer them to the nearest District Recruitment Center for induction into the relevant military contingents. There such men are immediately to take their basic training and shall be included in the next unit sent out to the front. If a worker so inducted is classified as fit for guard duty only, provision is to be made that after the completion of his basic training, he be assigned to a guard unit stationed in an area of military activity or in the immediate vicinity of such an area. For the Minister of War. Signed by his own hand, Major General Schleyer."

(*The Optimist is speechless.*)

GRUMBLER: You seem to be the one who is speechless now. You see that men who crave the blessing of being sent to the front are instead punished by being sent to the front.

OPTIMIST: Yes—even to intensify punishment!

GRUMBLER: Yes, indeed. The fatherland considers the opportunity of dying for the fatherland a punishment, the most severe punishment to boot. The citizen thinks of it as the highest honor. He wants to die a hero's death. He wants to enlist, but he is enlisted instead.

OPTIMIST: I cannot believe it—a punishment!

GRUMBLER: There are gradations of punishment. First disciplinary measures. Second, court proceedings. Third, intensification of jail sentence. And fourth, as the most severe intensification, the front. The incorrigibles are sent to the field of honor. The ringleaders! The repeat offender is sentenced to die the death of a hero. The hero's death is for the Chief of Staff a cruel blow of fate if his son suffers it, and the Minister of War calls it a punishment. Both are right. In both cases, the first words of truth that have been spoken in this war.

Act III

SCENE 2

In front of the Austrian artillery positions.

SCHALEK: Isn't that a simple man standing there, one who is nameless? He will be able to tell me in plain words about the psychology of war. It is his job to pull the cord on the mortar—seemingly a simple operation, and yet, what incalculable consequences are tied to this moment. Is he aware of it? Does he spiritually measure up to the sublimity of this task? Of course, those back home, who know nothing more about cord except that it threatens to run out, have no idea what kind of heroic opportunities are offered precisely to the simple man on the battle line who pulls the cord on the mortar. (*She turns to a Gunner.*) Just tell me, what kind of feelings do you have when you pull the cord? I mean, what are your thoughts when you fire the mortar? (*The Gunner looks startled.*) Well, what are your thoughts? Look, you're surely a simple man who is nameless. You must— (*The Gunner, taken aback, keeps silent.*) I mean, what do you think about when you fire the mortar? You must think of something. What is it you think about?

GUNNER (*after a pause, sizing her up from head to toe*): Nothing at all!

SCHALEK (*turning away in disappointment*): And he names himself a simple man. I'll simply not give the man's name.

(*She continues on down the front line.*)
(*Scene change.*)

SCENE 37

The Subscriber and the Patriot conversing.

PATRIOT: No bathroom at 10 Downing Street! What do you say to that!

SUBSCRIBER: What can I say? The walls are crumbling.

PATRIOT: No bathroom at Downing Street!

SUBSCRIBER: Well now, to whom do we owe this remarkable discovery? To him,* of course!

PATRIOT: Of course, but actually it was Mrs. Lloyd George who made this disturbing discovery, one has to admit that.

SUBSCRIBER: Well yes, that is true. But it was he who printed it.

PATRIOT: Well, and you know what follows then, with inescapable logic?

SUBSCRIBER: He writes expressly that the British Prime Ministers who have resided at 10 Downing Street for more than a century have either forgone the luxury of bathing or have been obliged to go to a public bath.

PATRIOT: Serves them right, those filthy people, I relish it.

SUBSCRIBER: And mind you, not the way it is here, because of the war—no, for more than a century they put up with that piggishness!

PATRIOT: Asquith lived there with his family for nine years.

SUBSCRIBER: That means he did not take a bath in nine years, neither he nor the whole family.

PATRIOT: Well now, one can't say that. Perhaps they went to a public bath.

* Moriz Benedikt.

SUBSCRIBER: I beg your pardon, nothing of the sort has ever been reported. Or did you ever read—

PATRIOT: Not that I can remember.

SUBSCRIBER: Well, there you are.

PATRIOT: But you know what is still possible? All right, there is no bathroom at Downing Street. All right, it is proven that they never went to a public bath—but from this it doesn't follow they never took a bath at all in a hundred years?

SUBSCRIBER: How come? Seems to me you're something of a skeptic!

PATRIOT: Look here, Mrs. Lloyd George discovered it, he writes, when they moved in. Now then, if she discovers such a thing—what will she do in the future?

SUBSCRIBER: Do I know? It's not my worry!

PATRIOT: She will do, I suppose, what most probably Mrs. Asquith also did.

SUBSCRIBER: Well, what did she do?

PATRIOT: What did she do? She did, I suppose, what most probably all of them did who lived there for a hundred years.

SUBSCRIBER: Well now, what did they do?

PATRIOT: What did they do? Well now, is there a bathroom at Schönbrunn?

SUBSCRIBER: At Schönbrunn? What do they have instead?

PATRIOT: Well—I have been told—I shouldn't be saying this —but let's suppose—well, has the Emperor not taken a bath for a hundred years or do you believe that he goes to the Central Baths?

SUBSCRIBER: Fine patriot you are! But what has that got to do with this—you better tell me what they did at Downing Street.

PATRIOT: What they did? Even a simple layman must realize

what they did. They told the shiksa to get water for them and they sent her for a tub. And there in the tub, they took their bath.

SUBSCRIBER (*stops his ears*): I can't bear to listen to such a thing. You're taking the last illusion away from a person.

PATRIOT: Pardon me, I'm just supposing. I believe he is right —they either did not take a bath at all then or were obliged to go to a public bath.

SUBSCRIBER: And I'm telling you they did not take baths at all. And that's all there is to it. Poincaré's position is shaken and Lloyd George humiliated. Englishmen and Germans will meet in Stockholm.

PATRIOT: What does this mean? What has that got to do with this? You almost strike me as if you were Old Biach.

SUBSCRIBER: Come on, that is something you really ought to know. That's how a lead article ends.

PATRIOT: Of course—I do know! You know what I think? The walls are crumbling.

SUBSCRIBER: You're telling me! In all the Allied countries, I've been told there are no bathrooms.

PATRIOT: No, that's exaggerated. Didn't you read about the tsarina in her bathtub?

SUBSCRIBER: Well yes, but as everybody knows, she had to share it with Rasputin.

PATRIOT: You know what I'm eager to know?

SUBSCRIBER: What? I'm eager to know.

PATRIOT: Whether there's a toilet at Downing Street. Or whether for the last one hundred years they were obliged to forgo the luxury or to utilize a public convenience. May God punish England!

SUBSCRIBER: We shall see what we shall see. (*Exit.*)

(*Scene change.*)

SCENE 42

*During the Battle of the Somme. Gate in front of a
villa. A company of front-line soldiers, wearing their
death-defying countenances, marches by into the foremost front-line trenches.*

CROWN PRINCE (*at the park gate, in a tennis outfit, waving to
them with his racket*): Do a good job!

(*Scene change.*)

SCENE 43

*The Ministry of War. A room fronting on the Ring-
strasse. A Captain sits at a desk. In front of him stands
a Civilian in deep mourning.*

CAPTAIN: Well, then, what more do you want? An up-to-date
report is an impossible thing in such cases. After all, we
can't know whether a man is dead or wounded and captured. You will have to go to the Italian ministry of war,
my dear fellow! Well, now then! What—in addition to
everything else are we supposed to do? It is simply unbelievable what people expect of us!

CIVILIAN: Yes—but—

CAPTAIN: My dear sir, I can tell you no more. Besides it is
almost three o'clock—you must have some understanding.
Office hours are over. That's really splendid—well, what
is it now? —Now then, off the record, I can tell you one

thing: you have heard nothing from your son now for six weeks; so confidently assume that he is dead.

CIVILIAN: Yes—but—

CAPTAIN: No but's about it. Where would we be if in such cases we—you can surely imagine that things like this occur a thousand times! There's a war on now, my dear sir! So the citizen must also do his part! Look at us who sit here! We stand here at our posts! And besides that, dear sir—as surely you do know—but again I say this to you privately and completely without any commitment on my part—that for a soldier there can be no higher ambition and no more beautiful reward than to die for the fatherland. So, it has been an honor—an honor—

(*The Civilian bows and leaves.*)

Act IV

SCENE 7

Physicians' meeting in Berlin.

PSYCHIATRIST: —gentlemen! This individual is the strangest case I have ever had. It was my lucky star that brought him to me from protective custody. Since it is obviously impossible to be sentenced to as many years of hard labor as this man would have to expect for his crimes, we had, whether we wanted to or not, to turn to psychiatry. Here for once we have a case where we need not ask whether the criminal is subjectively responsible for his crime; the deed itself is proof of his lack of responsibility. In order, gentlemen, to enable you to perceive fully the patient's irresponsibility for his actions, I need but mention that he voiced in public the opinion that the food situation in Germany was unfavorable! (*Restlessness.*) More than that: the man doubts Germany's final victory! (*Commotion.*) But, as though that were not enough, the man insists that unrestricted submarine warfare, and indeed submarine warfare

altogether, does not fulfill its purpose. It immediately became clear to me that he rejects this weapon as such,
and this not merely because he believes it does not fulfill
its purpose but because he regards it as downright immoral!
(*Shouts of excitement.*)

Gentlemen, we as men of science have the duty to maintain cool heads and to face the object of our indignation
only as an object of investigation, *sine ira* although *cum
studio*. (*Hilarity.*) Gentlemen, I comply with the sad duty
of sketching out for you a full picture of the mental confusion of the patient, and I must ask you to refrain from
placing the burden of responsibility on the shoulders of
this unfortunate individual or on mine, as I am no more
than the accidental demonstrator of a loathsome form of
insanity. His responsibility is canceled through his illness,
mine through science. (*Calls of "Right you are!"*)

Gentlemen, this man suffers from the fixed idea that
Germany is being driven toward an ultimate catastrophe
through a "criminal ideology," this being the term he uses to
refer to the sublime idealism of our country's rulers. He believes that we are lost unless we declare ourselves beaten,
although we are at the pinnacle of our victorious course. He
believes that it is our government, that it is our military
rulers—certainly not those of England (*shouts of "Hear,
hear"*)—who bear the blame for the fact that our children
will have to die! (*Cries of "For shame!"*) The mere assertion that our children will have to die, implying that our
food situation is unfavorable, alone suffices to demonstrate
beyond a shadow of a doubt the man's mental derangement.
(*Shouts of "That's right!"*)

I have presented this case to you, my highly esteemed
colleagues from internal medicine, so that you, gentlemen,
may attempt to exert an influence on the patient by con-
veying to him your experiences with regard to the state of

health of the German population in wartime. From the manner of his response I hope to obtain a rounding-out of the clinical picture, if not its rectification, toward an orientation in which criminal responsibility can perhaps still be demonstrated, since we must leave nothing untried—I hope then that the patient, under the impact of your authoritative exposition, will let himself be carried away into making such utterances that will make it easier for us to reach a decision in one direction or another. (*A voice from the audience: "We'll swing it!"*)

MENTAL PATIENT: If there is among you one of *the* ninety-three intellectuals,* I shall leave the hall! (*Shouts of "What insolence!"*)

PSYCHIATRIST: I trust, gentlemen, that you will take this outbreak less as an insult than as a symptom. I myself, as you all know, have signed that protest that will live on in the annals of our country as a milestone from a great age, and I am proud of it. I now ask our revered colleague Boas to undertake an experiment on the patient.

PROFESSOR BOAS (*stepping forward*): I have stated repeatedly and confirm once again that the health of our people has not been impaired by the restriction of available provisions. (*Shouts of "Hear, hear!"*) We can take it as an established fact that we have been getting along on no more than one-half the protein ration used before, without an adverse effect on our strength or fitness to work and, indeed, that we have even been able to increase our weight and to improve our physical well-being.

MENTAL PATIENT: You probably provide for your needs on the black market! (*Shouts of excitement.*)

---

* Refers to the leading German intellectuals who, at the beginning of the war, signed a proclamation supporting Germany's war aims.

PSYCHIATRIST: Gentlemen, consider the mental state of the man. Professor Boas, permit me to raise the question of infant mortality, which is a point that keeps coming up time and again in the imagination of our patient.

PROFESSOR BOAS: We have found that there can be no question of the food situation exerting an unfavorable influence on infant mortality.

MENTAL PATIENT: You mean, there *must* be no question— (*Shouts of "Shut up!"*)

PSYCHIATRIST: What do you anticipate, Professor Boas, from a continuation of the war?

PROFESSOR BOAS: With our increasing affluence and the concomitant increase in superabundant nutrition, we were squandering our national health. Now millions of our countrymen, under the pressure of privation, have learned to find the way back to nature and a simple way of life. Let us take care, gentlemen, that the lessons we are learning today in wartime will not again be lost to future generations. (*Shouts of "Bravo!"*)

MENTAL PATIENT: The man is quite right—the Kurfürstendamm crowd gorged too much before the war. But they are still eating too much. It is quite true that for them the food situation has not worsened at all. But as for the future generation of the rest of the population, those circles that do not consult Boas for obesity—for the future population of Germany I foresee children born with rickets! Children as invalids! Blessed are those who died during the war: those born during the war wear artificial limbs. I prophesy that the insanity of sticking it out and the miserable pride in the enemy's losses, which is as characteristic of German men as is the ardent eagerness of German Megaeras to have their sons die a hero's death—that this perverse state of mind of a society that breathes an air of organized glory and feeds on self-deception will leave behind a crippled Germany!

(*Shouts of "For shame!"*) As for this Boas, I challenge him to deny that up to now about 800,000 persons among the civilian population have died of starvation, that in 1917 alone some 50,000 more children and 127,000 more old men and women died than in 1913, that in the first six months of 1918 more Germans—approximately seventy percent more—died of tuberculosis than during the twelve months of 1913! (*Shouts of "Stop it! Stop it! Infamy!"*)

PSYCHIATRIST: You see, gentlemen, what condition this man is in. I thank our esteemed colleague Boas and will now call on our colleague Zuntz to undertake an experiment. I ask him to give his opinion on whether the German fitness to work, that most precious national asset, has suffered even in the minutest way as a result of nutrition.

PROFESSOR ZUNTZ: A reduction in the fitness to work, attributable to present nutrition, is out of the question. It is true that malnutrition has been brought about in wide circles of the population through the fact that the people don't like to ingest sufficient amounts of the less-concentrated vegetable foodstuffs.

PSYCHIATRIST: If I understand our esteemed colleague correctly, the population has itself to blame, for objectively there is no cause for malnutrition.

PROFESSOR ZUNTZ: No, there is none.

PSYCHIATRIST: But malnutrition, insofar as it is brought about or, let us say, if it is brought about at all, has no adverse consequences?

PROFESSOR ZUNTZ: None.

PSYCHIATRIST (*to the Mental Patient*): To this you have probably no answer?

MENTAL PATIENT: No, I don't.

PSYCHIATRIST: He has something insolent to say about everything, but here he is startled and holds his tongue! I thank our esteemed colleague Zuntz and now call on Rosenfeld-Breslau, whom it is our honor to welcome as the guest of the Berlin faculty, to undertake a test.

PROFESSOR ROSENFELD-BRESLAU: With all the malnutrition, our population has become healthier, and the great fear concerning the effects of malnutrition has proven to be unfounded. On the contrary: overeating in peacetime represents a greater danger to life than the food restrictions of the war years. Statistics have shown that almost all illnesses among the female population have resulted in fewer deaths during the war years than in peacetime. In any event, we can sum up our observations to the effect that wartime nutrition has not in any discernible measure reduced the people's resistance to the overwhelming majority of diseases, to illness, and to exertion.

MENTAL PATIENT: Except to the mendacity of professors! (*Vigorous shouts of indignation.*)

FIRST VOICE: Don't make a nuisance of yourself!

SECOND VOICE: Let's throw him out!

THIRD VOICE: We should get the police here!

CHAIRMAN OF THE SOCIETY OF PHYSICIANS OF GREATER BERLIN: I shall use the occasion of this scandal to raise my voice in a strong appeal. Colleagues: Each of you is the father confessor of your patients, it is your patriotic duty, by word of mouth and through any other form of action, in an enlightening and informative way, to encourage them to stick it out! You must take a most decisive stand against the fainthearted! Reject unfavorable and unfounded rumors that are often spread maliciously or thoughtlessly! We on the home front can, should, and will stick it out! Colleagues! The simple way of life, simpler food, moderation in the ingestion of proteins and fats, has proven conducive to the health of many.

MENTAL PATIENT: To profiteers and to physicians! (*Shouts of "Disgraceful! Out with him!"*)

CHAIRMAN: School physicians have incontestably established—

MENTAL PATIENT: —that Germany has successfully been bombarded with lies! (*Shouts of "For shame!"*)

CHAIRMAN: —that our children do not manifest impairment of health compared with former times!

MENTAL PATIENT: The increase in mortality amounts to only thirty-seven percent! (*Shouts of "Shut up! The man without a fatherland!"*)

CHAIRMAN: Infant mortality has declined. Only recently a leading authority has showed that the newborn have never done so well as now. (*Shouts of "That is correct!"*) The hospitals are less crowded than they were in the past.

MENTAL PATIENT: Because all are dead! (*Uproar.*)

VOICE: The fellow should prove that!

MENTAL PATIENT: The reports of many institutional physicians have a desperate ring when they describe the hunger of the inmates who try to devour thrown-away cabbage stalks and all sorts of indigestible refuse just in order to relieve their hunger pangs. A report requisitioned from a hospital reads laconically: All the inmates have died. —But those who are alive and assembled here have been ordered to issue expert opinions and will find the courage to speak the truth only after the unavoidable collapse of the lies, and of the Reich. But then it will be too late, and no confession will spare them the contempt of the rest of the world. For German science is a prostitute. Our men of science are its pimps! Those assembled here in order to deny—in the service of the General Staff's great lie—the dying of children and to make black look white bear a greater burden of blood guilt than those whose hands are bloody. Those ninety-three intellectuals who cried out "It is not true!" and "We protest!" opened the door to impassioned lies with their protest against attacks on German honor; and those who joined their ranks have drawn German culture even further away from Goethe and Kant and all good spirits of Germany than those romantic arsonists who forced them to lie.

(*Tremendous uproar. Shouts are heard of "It is not true!" and "We protest!" Several of the Professors are about to assault the Mental Patient but are held back by others.*)

PSYCHIATRIST: Gentlemen! We have just witnessed the most violent outburst of hatred of our fatherland, one that cannot possibly have grown on German soil. The patient's reaction to the experiments of our esteemed colleagues, Boas, Zuntz, and Rosenfeld-Breslau, and in particular, to the substantive and pellucid presentation of the esteemed Chairman of the Society of Physicians of Greater Berlin—for which I have to thank our esteemed colleague most warmly—has clearly proven to me that this man is not mentally disturbed but rather that he is in the pay of the Allies.

We are dealing here with an acute case of Northcliffe propaganda, the prevention of whose chronic dissemination is a special obligation of the medical profession of Greater Berlin. Even now the poison of pacifism has penetrated healthy brains, and the exaggerated idealism of the opponents to war encourages weaklings and draft dodgers to assume attitudes that must be seen as one of the worst evils from which the German national body suffers. If this is coupled with criminal propaganda, a condition is soon created that is apt to paralyze our initiative at a moment when ultimate victory is in sight. It is the spirit of defeatism that strengthens the enemy's backbone and lames our wings in a defensive war that has been forced upon us by

British envy (*a voice in the audience: "The British spirit of shopkeepers!"*), French thirst for revenge (*a voice in the audience: "And Russian rapacity!"*), and Russian rapacity.

Here for once we have a typical case before us. I cannot but emphasize that the man looked suspicious to me from the outset, and I have now come to the conclusion that we are dealing here with a real criminal. No mental patient speaks that way, gentlemen; he talks like a criminal enemy of the fatherland! I am in a position, gentlemen, to disclose, furthermore, that the man, through his unrepenting attitude during his protective custody, when he continued his outrageous attacks on everything that is sacred to us Germans and indeed allowed himself to be carried away to the point of speaking disapprovingly about the Wolff News Agency (*unrest*)—aroused the attention of the highest circles and that a personage venerable to all of us (*the audience rises*), our Crown Prince, voiced his opinion that this fellow should be punched in the nose. (*Shouts of "Hurrah!"*) It will depend on the decision of the respective highest authority as to whether such a remedy can be put to use, a remedy that possibly could be taken under advisement as an intensification of his punishment. It is incumbent upon us, gentlemen, to declare this matter outside of our province, since medical science has nothing to do with this case, and to refer the man to the care of the appropriate criminal agencies. (*Opens the door and calls.*) Officer!

POLICEMAN BUDDICKE (*entering*): In the name of the law—okay, come along now.

(*Exit with Mental Patient. The assembled physicians rise and intone "The Watch on the Rhine."*)

(*Scene change.*)

SCENE 11

A divisional command.

COMMANDER: Your Excellency, because of inadequate artillery support, this operation was hopeless. It was almost like target practice for the enemy to hit the pontoons we let down and their crews. Hundreds of bodies sank in the San that day, and then we had to give up the drive to cross the river anyway. We're facing the same situation now.

KAISERJÄGERTOD:* You must hold your ground at any cost.

COMMANDER: Your Excellency, the troops are freezing to death in trenches filled with icy ground water.

KAISERJÄGERTOD: How high do you estimate your probable losses?

COMMANDER: Four thousand.

KAISERJÄGERTOD: Your orders are to sacrifice the troops.

COMMANDER: When they come out of there, they'll be wading knee-deep in snow, and in addition, they are supposed to attack a superior enemy position.

KAISERJÄGERTOD: My God, don't you have any chaplain who could fire up the morale of the men? The offensive must not be delayed under any circumstances.

COMMANDER: Your Excellency, there's so much snow on the ground that a whole regiment will be wiped out.

KAISERJÄGERTOD: One regiment? What do I care about one regiment?

COMMANDER: These men are standing with empty bellies up

* Based on the name of the Kaiser Jäger Regiment; the added syllable means "death."

to here in water! They're fighting desperately against the powerful, uninterrupted assaults of the Russians.

(*Kaiserjägertod is called to the telephone.*)

KAISERJÄGERTOD: What? Relief or reinforcements? Colonel, you have to stand your ground to the last man; I have no troops at my disposal, and the word retreat doesn't exist for me, cost what it may! What? They want a day's rest to dry their clothes? What are you saying? Your poor brave Tyroleans are lying out there, shot to death and floating in the water? (*Bellowing.*) They're there to be shot! Period! —That's it, and I have nothing else to say to you. The troops absolutely must stick it out in their positions, my career is at stake! (*Exit.*)

MAJOR (*to the Commander*): There's nothing you can do, sir, His Excellency usually sends his crack troops in for the most difficult assignments exactly because of their outstanding qualities. His Excellency is an extremely energetic, purposeful, impulsive general who, himself brave and sternly demanding, requires unquestioning sacrifice from his subordinates.

(*Scene change.*)

SCENE 34

A police station.

DETECTIVE: Well, here's another one of those syphilitic little sluts. And is she full of lice!

PATROLMAN: Her I know. She did some time for petty larceny and she was also brought in for vagrancy. They've already had her at the clinic.

DETECTIVE: How old are you? Where are your folks?

SEVENTEEN-YEAR-OLD: Papa was drafted, and mother died.

DETECTIVE: How long have you been living this kind of life?

SEVENTEEN-YEAR-OLD: Since 1914.

(*Scene change.*)

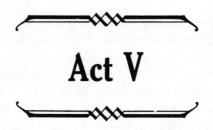

Act V

SCENE 33

The Optimist and the Grumbler conversing.

OPTIMIST: In order to gain insight into the emotional life of those fighting in the war one needs only—

GRUMBLER: —read a letter from the field—particularly, one from somebody who was able to slip it past the censor.

OPTIMIST: In any case, one would conclude from such letters that each man's greatest ambition is to give a good account of himself on the battlefield, and that his devotion to duty even takes precedence over his yearning for wife and child.

GRUMBLER: Or one would be horrified by the inconceivable crime perpetrated by the scoundrels who engendered the war and who are prolonging it—this inconceivable crime which is terrible enough in its effect on even a single destiny, but which is inflicted on millions—the tearing apart and trampling of every individual's happiness, the torture of expecting disaster for years, of a tension that trembles at the silence and dreads that it will be broken by a message of death from either the trenches or from the home front. A wife becomes a mother, a mother dies—and the man whom it most closely concerns lies in the mud somewhere for the sake of the fatherland. Now the scoundrels have contrived the ingenious arrangement whereby combat mail, this cursed and yet how much desired invention of Satan himself, is temporarily halted altogether. In such cases the poor wretches know more than enough; for the stillness is that which precedes the storm. And how unimaginable is the mechanism with which the elementary facts of life, birth, and death yield to the unfathomable decree of the general staff! Only love does not knuckle under. (*He reads aloud.*)

"—the common reason for the slowing up of the mail from here is said to be the fact that instead of censoring it they simply hold it back until events have overtaken the letters.

"I try in various ways to make this difficult, terrifying time easier for myself—all without success. If I think about you a lot, then I only get sadder still, and if I try to distract myself, then afterward I'm only still sadder. The best thing to do is to live one day at a time so that the time passes faster. For each day that passes does bring us closer together, we must not forget that!

"I am still overwhelmed by the concern I feel for you today, but I shall shake it off, and give myself wholly up to my hope for good news from you tomorrow. When I think that I could be with you now, see your beloved little face, talk with you about the days to come, days that will seal our happiness still more—and here I am, so far away, and you alone! Truly, this war is so cruel, so unnatural; let's not forget that we're not the only ones who have to suffer—so many, so innumerable are those who are made unhappy by the arbitrariness of a few unscrupulous men.

"But what do the others matter to me—it breaks my heart to think what we two have to go through right now! It is too terrible, hardly to be endured! And in addition one has to fulfill one's duty, difficult, heavy with responsibility, and dangerous as it is; one has to act as an example to one's men of courage and devotion to duty—and whatever else all these hateful virtues are called; each step I take in this whole affair is sickening and repulsive, is contrary to all my innermost convictions. We are required to disavow all our better feelings, and those unable to do so suffer unspeakably and do with disgust whatever is demanded of them, however sickening it may be.

"To think how happy we were, how our lives had become so entwined, so much one being that now one is completely lost without the other. I am so impoverished and small without you, sometimes you would hardly recognize me at all. So many times when I surrender to my thoughts, even when they're not just then flying out to you, I often want just to ask you something, to have you share something with me, to hear your opinion, and I am alone! I don't need anyone else's opinion, it's you I want to hear, it's for you that I think and feel, whatever the situation may be; and without you I am not myself, I am only half a person and destitute. Your love, which radiates out to me from afar, is the only thing that still preserves any joy in life for me.

"Why speak, why should I still exacerbate the wounds that burn so much even as it is. You know that you mean everything to me—or rather that you are the cause of my misery, for, if it were not for the thought of you, everything wouldn't be quite so bad! And sometimes I also think ahead to the future. To complete languor—half alive we shall lie in each other's arms and can do no more for love, love!

"Alas, that I can't be there! I wouldn't have moved from your side during the difficult hours that await you, and it would have been so much easier for you. Don't worry yourself about me. If I could magically spirit you to my side, I would quite calmly take you with me into the trenches.

"Oh, that I can't be with you! It's with you that I belong, and I can't be there. Oh, may God grant that you haven't suffered too badly, that nothing has happened to you, that you have remained well for me and that you will be getting stronger from day to day. Oh, may God grant that today I will get a postcard written in your own hand. By the time you receive these lines, you will, God willing, be all right. Did you feel that I was with you and that I was suffering along with you? Oh, the time will come—it has to come— when we will make it up to ourselves for all the suffering we've had to overcome.

"So far away, so far away from you, in these days! Oh, why, why, can't I sit by you now, to warm you and give you strength with my endless love! I can't help myself, my eyes are so full of tears all the time that I can hardly see what I'm writing.

"Oh God, that I can't be with you! And no hope! Nobody is sent home now or back to the base; they are only sent to some hospital.

"I've gotten so many gray hairs that I can't count them any more. But I love you, whether near or far, love, love, love, unspeakingly, maddeningly—"

OPTIMIST: What then? He'll return home and find a wife and child who are feeling just fine.

GRUMBLER: The fatherland has decreed differently. Here a human being comes into the world, there another falls. I have never read anything so sad or so true as this last letter of a man who became a father when he died.

(*Scene change.*)

SCENE 54

The Grumbler at his desk. He reads:

"The wish to establish the exact time that a tree standing in the forest needs in order to be converted into a newspaper has given the owner of a Harz paper mill the occasion to conduct an interesting experiment. At 7:35 he had three trees felled in the forest neighboring the factory, which, after their bark was scaled off, were hauled into the pulp mill. The transformation of the three tree trunks into liquid wood pulp proceeded so quickly that as early as 9:39 the first roll of newsprint left the machine. This roll was immediately taken by car to the printing plant of a daily newspaper four kilometers away; and no later than 11:00 A.M. the newspaper was being sold on the street. Accordingly, a time span of only three hours and twenty-five minutes was required in order that the public could read the latest news report on the material that stemmed from trees on whose branches the birds had sung their songs that very morning."

(*Outside, from quite far off, the cry:* "E-e-xtra—")

GRUMBLER: So it is five o'clock. The answer is here, the echo of my blood-haunted madness. And no longer does anything resound to me out of ruined creation except this one sound, out of which ten millions who are dying accuse me of still being alive, I who had eyes so to see the world, and whose stare struck it in such a fashion that it became as I saw it. If heaven was just in letting this come about, then it was unjust in not having annihilated me. Have I deserved this fulfillment of my deathly fear of life? What's looming there, invading all my nights? Why was I not given the physical strength to smash the sin of this planet with one ax blow? Why was I not given the mental power to force an outcry out of desecrated mankind? Why is my shout of protest not stronger than this tinny command that has dominion over the souls of a whole globe?

I preserve documents for a time that will no longer comprehend them or will be so far removed from today that it will say I was a forger. But no, the time to say that will not come. For such time will not be. I have written a tragedy, whose perishing hero is mankind, whose tragic conflict, the conflict between the world and nature, has a fatal ending. Alas, because this drama has no actor other than all mankind, it has no audience!

So you would have to continue to die for something, which you call Honor or the Bucovina province. For what have you died? Why this scorn of death? Why should you scorn that which you know not? To be sure, one scorns life, which one knows not. You first come to know it when the shrapnel has not quite killed you, or when the beast, acting on orders, foaming at the mouth, not long ago a man like yourself, throws himself on you, and you have a flash of consciousness on the threshold. And now the beast who commands you dares to say of you, you scorn death? And you have not used this moment to shout to your superior that he was not God's superior who could order Him to uncreate what was created? Oh, had you known, at the moment of sacrifice, about the profit that grows despite—no, with—the sacrifice, fattening itself on it! For never, until this indecisive war of the machines, has there been such godless war profit, and you, winning or losing, lost the war, from which only your murderers profited.

You, faithful companion of my words, turning your pure
faith upward to the heaven of art, laying your ear in tranquil
scholarship to its bosom—why did you have to pass into
the beyond? I saw you on the day when you marched out.
The rain and the mud of this fatherland and its infamous
music were the farewell, as they herded you into the cattle
car! I see your pale face in this orgy of filth and lies in
this frightful farewell at a freight station, from which the
human material is dispatched. Why could you not have died
just from experiencing this initiation, one that makes Wal-
lenstein's camp seem truly like the lobby of a palatial hotel!
For technological man becomes dirty before he gets bloody.
This is how your Italian journey began, you quester after art.

And you, noble poet's heart who, between the voices
of the mortars and the murderers, attended to the secret
of a vowel—have you spent four years of your springtime
beneath the earth in order to test your future abode? What
had you to seek there? Lice for the fatherland? To wait,
until the grenade splinter came? To prove that your body
can better resist the effectiveness of the Schneider-Creuzot
works than the body of a man from Torino can that of
the Skoda works? What, are we the traveling salesmen of
arms factories who are to testify to the superiority of our
firms, and to the inferiority of the competition, not with our
mouths but with our bodies?

Where there are many who travel, there will be many
who limp. So let them turn their sales areas into battlefields. But that they also had the power to coerce higher
natures into the service of wickedness—the devil never
would have dared to imagine such a consolidation of his
dominion. And had one whispered to him that in the first
year of the war, the war into which he had chased people,
hornbook in hand, in order that they transact his business

with more soul, if one had whispered to him that in that first year an oil refinery would reap a one hundred and thirty-seven percent net profit, David Fanto, seventy-three percent, Kreditanstalt Bank, twenty million, and that the profiteers in meat and sugar and alcohol and fruit and potatoes and butter and leather and rubber and coal and iron and wool and soap and oil and ink and weapons would be indemnified a hundredfold for the depreciation of other people's blood—the devil himself would have advocated a peace treaty that renounced all war aims.

And for that, you lay four years in dirt and damp, for that, the letter that wanted to reach you was obstructed, the book that wanted to comfort you was stopped. They wanted you to stay alive, for they had not yet stolen enough on their stock exchanges, had not yet lied enough in their newspapers, had not yet harassed people enough in their governmental offices, had not yet sufficiently whipped mankind into confusion, had not yet sufficiently made the war the excuse, in all their doings and circumstances, for their ineffectuality and their maliciousness—they had not yet danced this whole tragic carnival through to its end, this carnival in which men died before the eyes of female war reporters, and butchers became doctors of philosophy *honoris causa*!

You have lain weeks on end under the assault of mine throwers; you have been threatened by avalanches; you have hung by a rope, three thousand meters high, between the enemy barrage and the machine-gun fire of your own lines; you have been exposed to the ordeal, prolonged a hundred-fold, of the condemned; you had to live through the whole variety of death in the collision of organism and machine, death by mines, barbed wire, dumdum bullets, bombs, flames, gas and all the hells of curtain fire—all this because madness and profiteering had not vented on you enough of their cowardly spite. And you out there, and we here, are we supposed to stare still longer into the graves that we had to dig for ourselves by orders from highest quarters—as the old Serbian men were ordered to do, and for no other reason than that they were Serbs and still alive and therefore suspect!

Alas, if one were only—having got out of this adventure unscathed, although careworn, impoverished, aged—if one were only, by the magic of some divine retribution, granted the power to hold accountable, one by one, the ringleaders of this world crime, the ringleaders who always survive, to lock them up in their churches, and there, just as they did with the old Serbian men, to let each tenth one draw his death lot! But then not to kill them—no, to slap their faces! And to address them thus: What, you scoundrels, you did not know, you had no idea, that among the millions of possibilities of horror and shame, the consequences of a declaration of war, if it was so decided in the profiteers' war plans, would also be these: that children have no milk, horses no oats, and that even one far from the battlefield can go blind from methyl alcohol, if it has been so decided in the war plans of the profiteers? What, did you not conceive of the misery of one hour of a captivity that was to last for many years? Of one sigh of longing and of sullied, torn, murdered love? Were you not even capable of imagining what hells are opened up by one tortured minute of a mother's harkening into the distance, through nights and days of this years-long waiting for a hero's death? And you did not notice how the tragedy became a farce, became, through the simultaneousness of a new and hateful nuisance and a mania for fossilized forms, an operetta, one of those loathsome modern operettas, whose libretto is an indignity and whose music is torture?

What, and you there, you who have been murdered, you did not rise up against this order? Against this system of murder. Against an economic system that for all the future had to condemn life to sticking it out, to drop the curtain on all hope, and to relinquish to the hatred of nations the snatching of even the smallest bit of happiness? Outrages in war senselessly committed and outrages committed against everybody because there was a war on. Poverty, hunger, and shame piled up on those fleeing and those who could still stay in their homes, and all mankind shackled, within and without.

And statesmen in precipitous times called upon to their one duty, to curb mankind's bestial impulse—they have unleashed it! Cowardly hatred of life, inclined even in peacetime to kill animals and children, turned to the machine to ravish all that grows! Hysteria, protected by technology, overpowers nature; paper commands weapon. We were disabled by the rotary presses before there were victims of cannons. Were not all realms of imagination vacated when that manifesto declared war on all the inhabited globe?

In the end was the word. For the word that killed the spirit, nothing remained but to give birth to the deed. Weaklings became strong to force us under the wheel of progress. And that was the press's doing, the press alone, which with its whoring corrupted the world! Not that the press set the machinery of death into motion—but that it eviscerated our hearts, so we could no longer imagine what was in store for us: that is its war guilt! And from the lascivious wine of its debauchery all peoples have drunk, and the kings of the earth fornicated with the press. And the horseman of the apocalypse drank to it, he whom I saw galloping through the German Reich, long before he actually did so.

A decade has passed since I knew that his task was achieved. He is rushing ahead at full speed in all the streets. His moustache stretches from sunrise to sunset and from south to north. "And power was given to him that sat thereon to take peace from the earth, and that they should kill one another." And I saw him as the beast with the ten horns and the seven heads and a mouth like the mouth of a lion. "They worshipped the beast, saying, Who is like unto the beast? Who is able to make war with him? And there was given unto him a mouth speaking great things." And we fell through him and through the whore of Babylon, who, in all tongues of the world, persuaded us that we were each other's enemy, and there should be war!

And you who were sacrificed did not rise up against this scheme? Did not resist the coercion to die, did not resist the last liberty—to murder? All human rights and values traded for the idea of the material; the child in his mother's womb pledged to the imperative of hatred; and the image of this fighting manhood, yes, even of this nursing womanhood, armored bodies with gas masks, like those of a horde of mythical beasts, handed down to the horror of posterity. With church bells you fired on the devout, and before altars of shrapnel, you did not repent.

And in all that, glory and fatherland? Yes, you have experienced this fatherland, before you died for it. This fatherland, from that moment when you had to wait undressed in the sweaty and beery air of the entrance hall to the hero's death, while they inspected human flesh and forced human souls to take the most godless oaths. Naked you were, as only before God and your beloved, before a board of tyrannical martinets and swine! Shame, shame for body and soul should have made you deny yourself to this fatherland!

We have all seen this fatherland, and the luckier ones among us, who could escape it, saw it in the figure of the impudent border guard. We saw it in all shapes of the greed for power of the freed slaves, in the accommodativeness of the tip-greedy extorter. Only we others did not have to experience the fatherland in the shape of the enemy, the real enemy, who with machine guns drove you in front of the enemies' machine guns. But had we seen it only in the likenesses of these hideous generals, who, all through this time of greatness, publicized themselves in fan magazines, as expensive ladies do in peacetime, to show that people are not always only whoring, but are also killing—truly we longed for this blood brothel's closing hour!

What, you there, who were murdered, who were cheated, you did not rise up against this system? You endured the license and luxury of the press strategists, parasites, and buffoons, just as you endured your misfortune and your coercion? And you knew, that for your martyrdom they received medals of honor? And you did not spit this glory in their faces? You were lying in trains that carried the wounded, which the rabble were permitted to write up for their papers? You did not break out, did not desert for a holy war, to liberate us at home from the archenemy who daily bombarded our brains with lies? And you died for this business? Lived through all this horror, only to prolong our own, while we here groaned in the midst of profiteering and misery and the harrowing contrasts of bloated impudence and the voicelessness of tuberculosis.

Oh, you had less feeling for us than we had for you, we who wanted to demand back a hundredfold each hour of these years that they tore out of your lives, we who always had only one question to ask you: what will you look like when you have survived this! When you have escaped glory's ultimate goal—that the hyenas become tourist guides, offering the site of your graves as sightseeing attractions! To be ill, impoverished, dissolute, full of lice, famished, killed in battle in order for the tourist trade to increase—this is the lot of all of us! They have carried your hide to market— but even out of ours their practicality lined their money purse.

But you had weapons—and did not march against this home front? And did not turn around from that field of dishonor to take up the most honorable war, to rescue us and yourselves? And you, the dead, do not rise up out of your trenches to take these vipers to account, to appear to them in their sleep with the twisted countenances that you wore in your dying hour, with the lusterless eyes of your heroic waiting, with the unforgettable masks to which your youth was condemned by this regime of madness! So, rise up, and confront them as the personification of a hero's death, so that the cowardice of the living, empowered to command, might finally come to know death's features and look death in the eye for the rest of their lives. Wake their sleep with your death cry! Interrupt their lust by the image of your sufferings! They were able to embrace women the night after the day on which they strangled you.

Save us from them, from a peace that brings us the pestilence of their nearness. Save us from the calamity of shaking hands with army prosecutors who have returned home and of meeting executioners in their civilian occupations.

Help me, you who have been murdered! Come to my aid, so that I do not have to live among men who, out of ambition or self-preservation, gave orders that hearts should stop beating and that the heads of mothers turn white! As sure as there is a God, without a miracle there can be no salvation! Come back! Ask them what they have done with you! What they did, as you suffered through them, before you died through them! What they did during your Galician winters! What they did that night when telephoning command posts got no answer from your positions. For all was quiet on the front.

And only later they saw how bravely you stood there, man by man, rifle ready to fire. For you did not belong to those who went over to the enemy or to those who went behind the lines and who, because they were freezing, had to be warmed up with machine-gun fire by a fatherly superior officer. You held your positions and were not killed while stepping backward into the murderous pit of your fatherland. Before you the enemy, behind you the fatherland, and above you, the eternal stars! And you did not flee into suicide. You died, neither for, nor through, the fatherland, neither through the ammunition of the enemy, nor through ours—you stood there and died through nature!

What a picture of perseverance! What a Capuchins' Crypt! Arms-bearing corpses, protagonists of Hapsburgian death-life, close your ranks and appear to your oppressors in their sleep. Awaken from this rigor! Step forth, step forth, you beloved believer in the spirit, and demand your precious head back from them! And where are you, you who died in the hospital? From there they sent back my last greeting, stamped: "No longer here. Address unknown." Step forth to tell them where you are, and how it is there, and that you never again will let yourself be used for such a thing.

And you there, with the face to which you were condemned in your last minute, when the beast, acting upon orders, frothing at the mouth, maybe once a man like you, plunged into your trench—step forth! Not that you had to die—no, that you had to experience this is what henceforth makes all sleep and all dying in bed a sin. It is not your dying, but what you have lived through that I want to

avenge on those who have inflicted this on you. I have
formed them into shadows. I have stripped off their flesh!
But to their stupid thoughts, to their malicious sentiments
and the frightful rhythm of their nothingness, I have given
body and now make them move.

Had one preserved the voice of this era on a phonograph,
the outer truth would have been in conflict with the inner
truth and the ear would not have recognized either of them.
Thus, time makes the essential truth unrecognizable and
would grant amnesty to the greatest crime ever perpetrated
under the sun, under the stars. I have preserved this truth,
and my ear has detected the sound of their deeds, my eyes
the gestures of their speaking, and my voice, when it only
quoted, did so in such a way that the fundamental tone remains for all time.

> And let me speak to the yet unknowing world
> How these things came about: so shall you hear
> Of carnal, bloody, and unnatural acts,
> Of accidental judgments, casual slaughters,
> Of deaths put on by cunning and forced cause
> And in this upshot, purposes mistook
> Fall'n on the inventors' heads. All this can I
> Truly deliver.

And should the times hear no more, so surely will hear
a being above them! I have done nothing but abridge this
deadly quantity, which, in its immeasurability, may try to
exonerate itself by pointing to the fickleness of time and
the press. All their blood after all was only ink—now the
writing will be done in blood! This is the war. This is my
manifesto. *I have considered everything carefully.* I have
taken it upon myself to tell the tragedy, which breaks down
into the scenes of mankind breaking down, so that the
Spirit, which has compassion for the victims, would hear

it, even had he renounced for all future time any connection with a human ear. May he receive this era's fundamental tone, the echo of my madness haunted by blood through which I, too, am guilty of these sounds. May he accept it as redemption!

(*From outside, quite far off, the cry:* "*E-e-xtra, E-e-xtra!*")

(*Scene change.*)

APHORISMS

Aphorisms

An aphorism need not be true, but it should surpass the truth. It must go beyond it with one leap.

You cannot dictate an aphorism into a typewriter. It would take too long.

One who can write aphorisms should not waste his time writing essays. Aphorisms call for the longest breath.

It is often difficult to write an aphorism if one knows how to do it. It is much easier if one does not.

———

I speak of myself and mean the cause. They speak of the cause and mean themselves.

Why is it that so many people find fault with me? Because they praise me and I find fault with them nevertheless.

My public and I understand each other very well: it does not hear what I say, and I do not say what it would like to hear.

You wouldn't believe how hard it is to transform an action into a thought!

Through my satire I make unimportant people so big that later they are worthy targets of my satire, and no one can reproach me any longer.

I am already so popular that anyone who vilifies me becomes more popular than I.

The world wants one to be responsible to it, not to oneself.

It happened so often that one who shared my opinions kept the larger share for himself that I have learned my lesson, and now offer people merely thoughts.

To me it still is a greater miracle that a fly flies than that a human being flies.

I hear noises which others don't hear and which disturb for me the music of the spheres, which others don't hear either.

I have often been begged to be just and to view a situation from all sides. I have done this in the hope that a situation might be better looked at from all sides. But I came to the same conclusion about it. So I persist in viewing a situation from only one side, whereby I save myself much labor and disappointment.

If I knew for a fact that I might have to share immortality with certain people, I would prefer a separate oblivion.

My readers believe that I write just for the day because I write about the day. So I must wait until my writings are outdated. Then they may possibly achieve timeliness.

———————

Erotics is to sexuality what gain is to loss.

Eroticism is the overcoming of obstacles. The most tempting and most popular obstacle is morality.

Eroticism transforms a despite into a because.

It is not the beloved who is distant but distance is the beloved.

Love and art embrace not what is beautiful but what by that embrace becomes beautiful.

Woman's sensuality is the primary source in which man's mind finds renewal.

Man has channeled the torrent of woman's sexuality. It no longer inundates the land but neither does it fertilize it.

The seducer who boasts of initiating women into the mystery of sex is like a stranger who arrives at the railway station and offers to show the tourist guide the beautiful sights of a town.

There is no provision in law against a man who marries a young, innocent girl on the promise of seduction and when the victim consents has no further interest.

They treat a woman like a cordial. They do not want to accept the fact that women thirst.

Moral responsibility is what man is lacking when he demands it from women.

"That hateful man," she cried, "has given me a love child."

An unscrupulous painter who, on the pretext that he wanted to seduce a woman, lures her into his studio to paint her picture.

If a connoisseur of women falls in love, he is like a doctor who gets infected at the patient's bed. A vocational risk.

Man's superiority in love relations is a paltry advantage by which nothing is gained and only violence is done to woman's nature.

For her perfection only a flaw is missing.

She entered into marriage with a lie. She was a virgin and did not tell him.

If a man has not married a virgin, he is a fallen man; he is ruined for life and at the very least has a claim for alimony.

The ideal of virginity is the ideal of those who would ravish.

Jealousy is a dog's barking that attracts thieves.

If one does not derive pleasure from making gifts to a woman one should not do it. There are women compared with whom the filling of the Danaides' sieve is the merest money box.

There is no more unfortunate being under the sun than a fetishist, who longs for a woman's shoe and has to make do with a whole woman.

Cosmetics is the science of woman's cosmos.

He forced her to do her bidding.

It is the true relationship between the sexes when the man affirms: I think of nothing else but you and therefore always have new thoughts.

In man's love life complete disorder has come about. One finds mixed forms, the potentiality of which one had hitherto no idea. A Berlin female sadist was recently said to have let slip the words: "Wretched slave, I command you to slap my face at once!" Whereupon the young lawyer in question fled in terror.

The highest position of trust: to be a father confessor of uncommitted sins.

No boundary is so conducive to smuggling as the age boundary.

Vienna has beautiful surroundings to which Beethoven often fled.

———

Come on, don't be a bore, says the Viennese to anyone who is bored in his company.

Suggestions as to how to lure me back to this city: change the dialect and prohibit procreation.

When someone has behaved like an animal, he says: "I am only human." But when he is treated like an animal, he says: "I, too, am a human being."

That we all are only human, is no excuse but a presumption.

I found somewhere the notice "It is requested that you leave this place as you would wish to find it." If only philosophers would speak half so impressively to mankind as hotel owners!

Often even I sense something like a presentiment of love for mankind. The sun smiles, the world is young again, and if on this day someone asked me for a light, I would be tempted, I almost think, I wouldn't let him ask long, and would give him one.

A cigar, said the altruist, a cigar, my dear fellow, I cannot give you. But if you ever need a light, just come round; mine is always lit.

A country horse will sooner get accustomed to a motor car than a passer-by on the Ringstrasse. There have already been many accidents through shying.

I know a country where the slot machines rest on Sunday, and do not work during the week.

Nationalism is the love that ties me to the fatheads of my country, the insulters of my moral sense, the profaners of my language.

Curses on the law! Most of my fellow citizens are the sorry consequences of uncommitted abortions.

The devil is an optimist if he thinks he can make people worse.

———————

Psychotherapy: When one is in good health, he can best be cured of that condition by being told what illness he has.

Psychoanalysis is that mental illness for which it regards itself as therapy.

One of the most common illnesses is the diagnosis.

The psychoanalyst is a father confessor who lusts to listen also to the sins of the father.

Medicine: Your money and your life!

He died from the bite of the Aesculapian serpent.

———————

Christian morality prefers remorse to precede lust, and then lust not to follow.

Christianity has enriched the erotic meal with the hors d'oeuvre of curiosity and spoiled it with the dessert of remorse.

It puzzles me how a theologian can be praised because after long inner struggles he has made up his mind not to believe in dogma. True recognition, as for a heroic deed, always seemed to me due the achievement of those who have struggled to the conclusion to believe in dogma.

Language is the mother of thought, not its handmaiden.

Language the mother of thought? Thought not the merit of the one who thinks? Oh, surely he must impregnate language.

What lives of subject matter, dies of subject matter. What lives in language, lives by language.

My language is the common prostitute that I turn into a virgin.

I master only the language of others. Mine does with me what it will.

The closer one looks at a word, the farther away it moves.

Why do some people write? Because they do not have enough character not to write.

Word and essence—the only connection I ever sought in my life.

A love affair that did not remain without consequences. He presented a work to the world.

The dog sniffs first, then he lifts his leg. One cannot well object to this lack of originality. But that the writer reads first, before he writes, is pitiful.

Despise people who have no time. Have compassion for those who have no work. But those who have no time for work, they are worthy of our envy!

It is a pitiful sort of mockery that expends itself in punctuation—employing exclamation marks, question marks, and dashes as if they were whips, snares, and goads.

The most dangerous writers are those whom a good memory relieves of all responsibility. They cannot help having things come flying to them. I would prefer an honest plagiarist.

Many talents preserve their precocity right into their old age.

Young Jean Paul's plan was to write books so that he could buy books. The plan of our young writers is to get books as gifts so that they can write books.

If Mr. Shaw attacks Shakespeare he acts in justified self-defense.

Today's literature is prescriptions written by patients.

No ideas and the ability to express them—that's a journalist.

Journalists would like to be writers. Collections of columns are published at which one looks with nothing more than astonishment that the work has not fallen apart in the hands of the bookbinder. Bread is baked from crumbs. What is it that leads them to hope for permanence? The on-going interest in the subject which they "choose" for themselves. When one prattles about eternity, should he not be heard for as long as eternity lasts? Journalism lives on this fallacy. It always has the greatest themes, and in its hands eternity can become topical; but it must also become obsolete again with equal ease. The great writer fashions the day, the hour, the minute. However limited and conditioned in time and place his cause may be, his work grows the more boundless and free the further it is removed from the incident; don't worry about its going out of date now; it will become current again in decades to come.

———

That a work is artistic need not necessarily prejudice the public against it. One overestimates the public in thinking that they resent stylistic excellence. They pay no attention whatsoever to style and unhesitatingly accept what is of lasting value provided that the subject happens to appeal to a vulgar interest.

You must read all writers twice, the good and the bad. You will recognize the former and unmask the latter.

I know of no heavier reading than light reading. Fantasy strikes against matter and dissipates too soon to keep on working spontaneously. One rushes through the lines, in which a garden wall is described, and the mind lingers on an ocean. How enjoyable the spontaneous voyage would be if at not just the wrong time the rudderless ship is once more dashed to pieces against the garden wall. Heavy reading presents dangers one can overlook. It strains one's own energy, while the other releases energy and leaves it to itself. Heavy reading can be a danger to weak energy. Strong energy is a danger to light reading. The mind must be a match for the former; the latter is no match for the mind.

How is it that I have all the time not to read so much?

Writing a novel may be pure pleasure. Experiencing a novel is not without difficulty. But reading a novel I guard against as best I can.

I haven't tried it yet, but I believe I would first have to coax myself and then close my eyes fast to read a novel.

Much knowledge has room in an empty head.

An illusion of depth often occurs if a blockhead is a muddle-head at the same time.

One shouldn't learn more than what one absolutely needs against life.

I saw a terrible apparition: An encyclopedia walked toward a polyhistor and looked him up.

The value of education is most clearly revealed when educated people begin to speak on a problem that lies outside the sphere of their competence.

Education is what most receive, many pass on, and few possess.

It has been said that I had tried to reduce him to a nonentity. That's not true. I only succeeded.

I once knew a hero who reminded you of Siegfried because of the thickness of his skin and of Achilles because of the peculiarity of his heel.

After he had made his position among the Anarchists untenable, there remained no alternative for him other than to become a useful member of bourgeois society and join the ranks of the Social Democrats.

What are all the orgies of Bacchus compared to the intoxications of one who surrenders himself to unbridled abstinence!

My son is not doing well. He is a mystic.

The words "family ties" have a flavor of truth.

Thoughts are duty-free. But they do cause you trouble.

Progress celebrates Pyrrhic victories over nature.

There is no gratitude to technology; it has to invent.

The secret of the demagogue is to appear as stupid as his audience so that it can believe itself to be as smart as he.

War is at first the hope that things will get better for oneself; after that the expectation that things will get worse for the other; then satisfaction that things are no better for the other; and after that astonishment that things are going badly for both.

Social policy is the despairing decision to undertake a corn operation on a cancer patient.

POEMS

FROM EARLY DAYS

It can ne'er other be.
No longer does my faith a shadow throw.
From thine unending light its radiant glow
Came from thy sex's shining mystery.

Now I am all in light,
That gently gleams o'er my unworthy head.
So long has all my faith in God been dead.
His very visage now fulfills my sight.

How it dispels all doubt!
How art thou, dearest, clear to me at last.
How do I clasp thee in thy heaven fast!
How doth this earthbound world thy value flout.

How shines thy splendor bright.
He holds thy being close, who longs to pray.
He hallows with his kiss. How veiled are they,
The stars, in this, of all, thy deepest night.

It ne'er shall other be.
Although all earthly things return to soil,
Thy ruin alone a heavenly bliss would spoil.
Yield not to earth, remain for ever thee!

TRANSLATED BY D. G. WRIGHT

TO THE AFFLUENT

That they live in sorry darkness,
That all sunshine beams on you;
That for you they lift the burdens,
Bearing their own burden too;
That you're free just through their fetters,
That their night your day has brought:
What from guilt will bring your rescue,
That you spared them ne'er a thought!

TRANSLATED BY D. G. WRIGHT

PARK LAWN
(Schloß Janowitz)

How time is vanished. Facing the past, I stand
spellbound, fast-rooted in the meadow-lawn,
as in the emerald mirror there, the swan.
And this my Holy Land.

These many bluebells! Gaze and hearken you!
How long he lingers there upon the bough,
that admiral-moth. It must be Sunday now,
and all the world rings blue.

I'll stray no farther. Idle footstep, hold!
Before this wonder let your wandering cease.
A dead day's eyes unveil upon this peace.
And all remains so old.

TRANSLATED BY ALBERT BLOCH*

* The translations by Albert Bloch included in this section were
first published in 1930.

MY CONTRADICTION

When life with lying falsehood they afflicted,
I was a revolutionary.
When norms unnatural they on us inflicted,
I was a revolutionary.
With those who suffered I have shared the torment.

When freedom was a phrase of emptiness,
I was a reactionary.
When art they tarnished with their craftiness,
I was a reactionary.
And have gone back to the very first elements.

TRANSLATED BY D. G. WRIGHT

TRANSFORMATION

Voice in the Fall, renouncing over the grave
all your world, pale sister, you, of the moon,
sweetest betrothed of the wind in its wailing
wafting beneath the scurrying stars—

swept thee aloft to thyself the cry of the spirit?
brought a desert storm thee back to thy life?
Lo, so guides God a first human pair
back again to the hallowed island!

Now it is springtime. Quivering herald of bliss,
through the world's winter came the butterfly golden.
Oh kneel you, and bless, hear, how the earth is still.
She alone knows of sacrifice and sorrow.

TRANSLATED BY D. G. WRIGHT

HOUR OF THE NIGHT

Hour of the night time, fleeing from me,
While I'm conceiving, reflecting, and weighing,
Soon will this night come to its ending.
Outside a song bird trills: it is day.

Hour of the night time, fleeing from me,
While I'm conceiving, reflecting, and weighing,
Soon will this winter come to its ending.
Outside a song-bird trills: it is spring.

Hour of the night time, fleeing from me,
While I'm conceiving, reflecting, and weighing,
Soon will this life span come to its ending.
Outside a song bird trills: it is death.

TRANSLATED BY D. G. WRIGHT

FALLING ASLEEP

What may befall me now?
Why do I dread this change?
I shall see something strange.
I know not what nor how.

I know not what it means,
yet feel it creeping nigh.
How to evade its eye!
Now at my heart it leans.

O lost delight unfound!
Oh if this hour might stand!
Oh might the hour's hand
begin anew its round!

Away with all the clocks!
Time ticks within my heart.
The flickering candles start.
The secret darkness mocks.

Oh let there be delay!
O secret, speak your terror.
Batter me down that mirror!
I will not be its prey!

Sleep, rescue me from death.
From life Oh let me borrow.
Bring once again the morrow.
Now lull me in your breath.

A face leans out and smiles,
and by some touch transforming,
new shapes come round me swarming,
and everything beguiles.

This all was long ago.
Now is the burden mild.
Why, I was once a child!
How springtime's blossoms blow.

So vision fades in night.
Now visions come, a bright rout.
And when I put the light out
all darkness will be light.

New faith at last is mine.
Soon consciousness will wane.
I am at peace again.
I have received a sign.

TRANSLATED BY ALBERT BLOCH

THE DYING MAN

The Man

Now it's enough. It's brought no joy as yet,
And now there's nothing new that can be tendered.

Conscience

Your life within the hour must be surrendered,
And you've shown no repentance, no regret.

The Man

For things one's done remorse can only be.
I gave no promise and have nought accomplished.

Memory

I helped you pass the time. And so years vanished
As weeks, you must agree. Just look at me!

The Man

I always looked behind, and you were there,
And were you not, I closed my eyes so gladly.

The World

I seemed within your world to serve you badly.
You only saw the distant ever near.

The Man

And all that's near, afar! Just leave mind's realm alone!
Don't interfere. I can show best what you are.

The Spirit

If the world torments you, why do you lend your ear?
You have from me, not her, all that you know!

The Man

How know I what I know! I do not know.
I think, I doubt, I hope, I fear, I tremble.

Doubt

When I uplift you, friend, you will not stumble.
Your faith in my true countenance bestow.

The Man

I know you well, you have through many a night
made it hot for me and many a word dissected.

Faith

But I, believe me, always with you sided,
Fanned with my breath the embers to ignite.

The Man

Too much, alas, too deep my soul was burned.
Oft 'twas like hell and oft like lightning's stroke.

Wit

I'm right at hand. I'm Wit, and that's no joke.
It's me in earnest, yet as jest mistaken.

The Man

Who would be what he is, when life so varies
Deceit and truth in such pathetic rote!

The Dog

I'm just a dog, and cannot read the dailies.

The Burgher

I am the boss and liberals have my vote.

The Prostitute

I, being a woman, by the world am tarnished.

The Burgher

Not being a man, in world esteem attired.

The Man

For worldly honor I have never languished,
And world's love has left me uninspired.

God

Walking in darkness you did see the light.
Now you are here and look into my face.
You looked behind yourself and sought my garden.
At the source you stayed. The source, it is the goal.
You, unsurrendered to life's sullying game,
No longer do you have to wait, my child.

TRANSLATED BY D. G. WRIGHT

RIME

Note: The omission of a stanza of the original is indicated by a line of ellipses.

Rime comes but by the word's high favor,
and not through art as added savor.

Well-born within its proper place,
the fruit of two ideas' embrace.

It is no arbitrary thing,
idly through forms meandering.

It is a content, not a dress,
much liked today, tomorrow less.

Not ornament of vanity,
nor solemn pomp's inanity.

It is no spice, it is a food;
no light o' love—it must be wooed.

It is the shore fixed for their landing,
when two thoughts reach an understanding.

It is so deep or is so shallow
as feeling is mature or callow.

It is as trite or full of worth
as is the thought that gave it birth.

It is as new and is as old
as is the poem's perfected mould.

The rime of Orphic song—I know it!—
the comic opera too can show it.

While words their ancient worth retain,
old rimes grow ever young again.

Beats in the verse a pulse, a heart,
then must pulsate the rime with smart.

. . . .

Here guides a word to regions far:
O wondrous union with a star!

. . . .

The word, to whom its grace is sent,
is miracle and sacrament.

Too often but a sugary glue,
the rime is verse's honeydew.

Here nature offers up her treasure,
there technique, cheaper sweeter pleasure.

True to themselves, words cannot lie,
yet will they lead false taste awry.

There tone with tone is merely blent,
here lives it in its element.

. . . . . .

There rime conceals the inner rift
and as a verse-foot crutch makes shift.

Here it is bound up in the whole:
The poet's bond—the verse's soul—,

more closely still to bind what's bound.
Not to be sought, but only found;

what to the word's high lot bears witness,
and not by featness, but by fitness

exists and of itself succeeds,
straight from the womb of language speeds:
that's rime—and not your jingling screeds!

TRANSLATED BY ALBERT BLOCH

WHEN BOBBY DIED
(February 22, 1917)

The great big dog is dead. Oh heart, stand still,
That this sad news my inner mind may fill!

The lordly eye, the silent godhead's pawn,
The light of loving now alas is gone.

How peacefully he lived apart from strife,
Worthily, wisely, he strode his way through life.

We others on faith's grave our lives we lead.
That others were, his eyes showed thanks indeed.

Whene'er his mistress called, oh pleasure sweet!
What glad excitement, sleeping by her feet.

Yet ere he slept, his majesty the hound
Must turn himself in circles round and round.

And when he found a fitting resting place
He then had many enemies to face.

There is no word, no handclasp, apt to draw
From heart to heart such trust as this good paw.

He never hid his thoughts from us, the hound,
He was so zealous, if some fault were found:

And when he failed, he truly was distressed,
Wagging his tail his honesty impressed.

In gratitude he used to dance before us,
His soul would sicken with desire so zealous.

I call to him through all eternity:
He starved whenever he was far from me!

Since fate has now reversed our situations,
He's taught us much of yearning's tribulations.

So let it be inscribed in words so tearful:
He's gone, and we are left behind and mournful!

Each hour that strikes is emptier than before,
Now that, great dog, you're silent ever more.

TRANSLATED BY D. G. WRIGHT

I SAW A GLIMMER IN AN EYE

I saw a glimmer in an eye this day,
and never shall escape it till I die.
Does not this guilt-stained earth quake in dismay,
now I have seen this glimmer in an eye?

Upon a highway's edge, dust-blown, dust-born,
in springtime all-too pitifully flowered,
there stands a bush amid a world forlorn,
on which God fruitlessly His blessings showered.

And there before the bush a woman stood,
and I stood too and only saw her glance.
O how it pierced me! How its quiet mood
did hold me rooted there in awestruck trance.

That countenance in its emaciation,
that glance, so poor, so dimmed with work and pain—
before so much of earthly abnegation
the whole world suddenly blooms green again!

Whatever happiness life might withhold,
however great this heart's long sacrifice,
it is repaid; before that glance so old,
the tattered shrub becomes a paradise.

No gardener heeds more tenderly his hedges
than this last sunset glimmer of this gaze.
No star smiles down more gently-wise its pledges
on love fulfilled in secret sacred maze.

I saw a glimmer in an eye this day,
and never shall escape it till I die.
Does not this guilt-stained earth quake in dismay,
now I have seen this glimmer in an eye?

TRANSLATED BY ALBERT BLOCH

BEFORE A FOUNTAIN
(Villa Torlonia)

What force the water's leap compels!
It soars and settles, sinks and swells;
it stands a stream, then falls downhurled,
commingling with its dewy world,

that, aimless from creation's day,
but lives to pour its life away,
and from its store abundantly
flouts duty's cold inclemency.

Before that Power alone it bends
who gave it being—to heaven ascends
its thanks-offering into the air,
a surging hymn of praise and prayer.

It seethes and surges, swirls and sings,
in blissful heedlessness it flings
and falls aloft, a toppling wave—
cold is the sun and hot the grave.

And as it lives in that it dies,
comes light to woo the watery prize.
The mind, cheered by such amours gay,
owes thanks now for a rainbow play!

What though the vessel overflow,
though all gush forth to nothing so:
the mind that views it still must gain,
what though delight and time must wane.

Nothing remains, yet all abides;
merged in the Holy Ghost it hides,
Who from the Fountainhead outpours:
through Him the holy line endures.

The fountain plays; its mystic rune,
from rapturous shout to plaintive croon,
sings, rising, falling, gleaming white,
in pity for man's sorry plight,

whose love, to merest use debased,
was killed and all its light effaced,
whose very life himself defamed,
shrinking from it, afraid, ashamed.

Still flows a stream, still flames a light,
still into song they dare unite;
still yearning mounts precipitate,
still opens wide a heavenly gate—

still on that rainbow I with you
had nearly passed beyond the blue,
that our love flow on timelessly,
O wondrous superfluity!

TRANSLATED BY ALBERT BLOCH

TO AN OLD TEACHER
(Henricus Stephanus Sedlmayer)

I saw you lately, as if the past were now,
Your head so white, and you
Looking somewhere for a word
That some poor pupil had lost.

Another, not ready to be called on
Had to find the word before finding himself.
And if he too were unable to do so
A callous sin was what you named it.

Instruction was quite tender and yet firm
You, good teacher, liked the pupil well.
Yet surely closer to your heart's purity
Lay the care for some poor word.

Latin and German, these to me you imparted.
But German I owe you, because I Latin had learned.
How German all became to me when I
Could read your beloved Ovidius.

For that truly caused me difficulty
I lacked words, and succeed I could not
In writing the required paper on spring
That I was only then just experiencing.

Ovid himself could hardly have done it,
and Goethe would have needed more than an hour.
How could a schoolboy have done it
Had he not happened to be a journalist?

You, kindly teacher, knew that only too well.
You showed forebearance, and because in Latin
I stood the test so very well,
You did not want to fail me in German.

So I passed, and later I did improve
Because I felt that I owed it to you
To live up to your expectations
In writing German essays after school days.

Had I already then between eight and nine
Written German as I read Latin
During the hour between ten and eleven
This Horacian ode would not have been wrought.

Accept this industry as salutation from my youth,
For you still stand before my mind's eye, as of old.
In image and in word you are near to me,
As if I sit before you still today.

I see you still, as with your gentle hand
You touch your brow that cares,
As if you must attend an ailing word
Sacred duty before witnesses profane.

Snow-white as then, your head inclined,
But high-minded as ever, I met you on the way
To school the other day; and so it was
As if I went along to school with you.

Where did dissolve your vista of the past?
Not lost to me.—Do you still teach
Language to the present, which is lost?
Take my advice and flunk the class!

TRANSLATED BY D. G. WRIGHT

BENEATH THE WATERFALL

Whoever before me had himself been blessed
by this cascade and by these sunbeams!
Who stood, with head in cosmic All,
proud on eternity's lofty shoreline!

For God has hither invited me
as high in grace as every beast,
and here is no one else but me,
freed from myself, myself I'll be.

What I myself created, embraces not myself,
woman and word, they pointed to the shadow.
And all my life was only tired, shallow,
my worldly course back to myself had flown.

Now home again to wonders that await me
and in God's world I'm all alone,
this sunbeam here is all my own.
How festively creation has embraced me!

Joy without suffering, love that's not oppressed,
and nature free of shame and limit—
To God's rich table I am come as guest
and to myself no more indebted!

Far behind me is all the woe and weakness.
How constant is the waterfall!
How does this sunny land bless all
my crowding thoughts before night's darkness

TRANSLATED BY D. G. WRIGHT

Selected Bibliography

Daviau, Donald G. "The Heritage of Karl Kraus." *Books Abroad* 38 (1964): 248–256.

————. "Language and Morality in Karl Kraus's *Die letzten Tage der Menschheit*." *Modern Language Quarterly* 22 (1961): 46–54.

Field, Frank. *The Last Days of Mankind: Karl Kraus and His Vienna*. New York: 1967.

Heller, Erich. "Karl Kraus: The Last Days of Mankind." *The Disinherited Mind*. New York: 1957.

————. "Dark Laughter." *New York Review of Books*, May 3, 1973, pp. 21–25.

————. "Satirist in the Modern World." *Times Literary Supplement*, May 8, 1953.

Janik, Allan, and Toulmin, Stephen. "Language and Society: Karl Kraus and the Last Days of Vienna." *Wittgenstein's Vienna*. New York: 1973.

Kerry, Otto. *Karl-Kraus-Bibliographie*. Munich: 1970.

Kohn, Caroline. *Karl Kraus: Le polémiste et l'écrivain, défenseur des droits de l'individu*. Paris: 1962.

Kraft, Werner. *Karl Kraus: Eine Einführung in sein Werk und eine Auswahl.* Wiesbaden: 1952.

———. *Karl Kraus: Beiträge zum Verständnis seines Werkes.* Salzburg: 1956.

Liegler, Leopold. *Karl Kraus und sein Werk.* Vienna: 1920.

Stern, J. P. "Karl Kraus's Vision of Language." *Modern Language Review* 61 (1966): 71–84.

———. "Karl Kraus and the Idea of Literature." *Encounter,* August 1975, pp. 37–48.

Weigel, Hans. *Karl Kraus oder die Macht der Ohnmacht.* Vienna: 1968.

Zohn, Harry. *Karl Kraus.* New York: 1971.